PROUD
FLESH

A Memoir

PROUD FLESH

The Resurrection of Baby B

CYNTHIA BOWEN

gatekeeper press

This is a true story. However, some names have been altered
to protect privacy.

Published by Gatekeeper Press
3971 Hoover Rd. Suite 77
Columbus, OH 43123-2839

ISBN: paperback 9781619844452
eISBN: 9781619844469

Printed in the United States of America

*To my husband Lawrence the family
we created and to all those who adopt to create
new families.*

Contents

PART III: Home

Prologue

MOST PEOPLE WHO hear my story tell me they could not have done what I did, *would* not have done what I did. They tell me they would not have been brave enough. "I don't know how you do it," they say. "I don't have that kind of patience," they lament. But perhaps they are too polite to say what they really think. The subtext: "I would never be foolish enough to do something like that." I am embarrassed; I squirm beneath their compliments and personal confessions. The pain is still too fresh. I still feel unsteady. Unworthy. What if I had failed? For a long time nothing I did seemed enough. Before Baby B, their words would have been my words. My life is divided into two parts: Before Baby B (B.B.) and After Baby B (A.B.)

Some even speak of the blessings I will receive in this life or the next. I am a woman of faith and will eagerly accept all blessings sent my way. However, I believe that blessings come as a result of God's grace alone and not as a byproduct of good works, good intentions, or good connections. I appreciate people's acknowledgment that what my family and I did was not easy. But the truth is, comments like this always leave me slightly perplexed and a little uneasy as I search for a response. I am an ordinary person who was living an ordinary life when I became part of another's extraordinary life.

If I had been able to think of myself as special or as someone possessing magical powers, I could have saved myself a lot of sleepless, nightmarish nights and anxious days wondering if I was up to the task. I certainly didn't think of myself as brave. I have always been a little bit shy and cautious almost to the point of cowardice. I practice patience only by continually monitoring an internal dialogue to stay calm and wait things out.

It helps me to remember what Dr. Martin Luther King, Jr. said: "The ultimate measure of a man is not where he stands in moments of comfort and convenience but where he stands at times of challenge and controversy." The enormity of what I had agreed to do did not occur to me until much later. I know, however, that I did not offer myself up out of some superior obligation to humankind or some vague altruistic urge to "give back." I never envisioned my involvement as some earnest endeavor to "Do good works," though I certainly saw the value in all of those things.

In the end, our family's love for Baby B drove everything to this conclusion: "Love never fails."

". . . see how the flesh grows back across a wound, with great vehemence, more strong than the simple, untested surface before.

"There's a name for it on horses, when it comes back darker and raised: proud flesh, as all flesh is proud of its wounds, wears them as honors given out after battle, small triumphs pinned to the chest. . . ."

—Jane Hirshfield, from *For What Binds Us*

PART I

B.B.B. (Before Baby B)

CHAPTER 1

Swept Along

"Some people come into our lives, leave footprints on our hearts, and we are never ever the same."

—*Eleanor Roosevelt*

July 2005

WHAT IF YOUR good deed turned into a lifetime commitment? What if your heart collided with commonsense warnings radiating like flashing red lights at a railroad crossing? What if at each turn along the twisting tracks you were given the chance to turn around, turn back, turn away? Instead you moved forward, unsteady, unsure, and afraid. Last but not least, what do we owe to people we don't know?

"Come closer, Mom," said my daughter.

I had come to Shriners Hospital on Galveston Island to meet Baby B for the first time. I took a step forward. The oversized polyester gown I pulled from the bin outside the door and slipped into gave off a soft "swish" sound when I moved. The gown was supposed to act as a shield against the world's germs.

Someone handed me a pair of disposable gloves. My hands felt sweaty and hot in them. Inching forward, I felt a suspended, floating sensation. I stood close to the corner of the bed and watched as Kanika untangled a tube and talked with the nurse. My eyes focused on the foot of the bed, then inched up little by little, back and forth across the bed like a computer, scanning. The tight corners of the bedsheets were tucked under, Girl Scout style. *Did little girls still earn sheet and diaper-folding badges? Probably not.* Bed rails, like prison bars, banked each side of the bed. An off-white blanket lay loosely across the sheets. About three-fourths up, the outline of a small shape took form under the covers. I hesitated. The room was filled with the steady beep-beep of monitoring machines recording the beat and pulse of a life.

I recalled the face of the little girl I had spoken to in the elevator minutes earlier. She was pressed against her mother, the sides of their bodies interlocked like puzzle pieces. They bunted their backs against the wall as if they feared a step forward might throw them into the bowels of the elevator. I smiled at the child and said hello to the woman. She softly replied, "*Hola*," looked down at the girl, and adjusted her pink jewel cap. The little girl glanced at me and tucked her chin into herself. Burn scars disfigured half her face, giving it a molten candle effect.

"That's a pretty pink cap you're wearing," I offered. The mother said something in Spanish to the child, who nodded and continued to look down. They made a silent exit at the next floor. I reviewed my words, hoping I hadn't insulted the child's intelligence. How many others had searched for something else to compliment besides her face?

As I stood beside the hospital bed, I tried to remember bits and pieces of previous conversations with my daughter. I had never considered the possibility that Baby B's face might be severely scarred, perhaps because I felt fairly confident that

Kanika would have prepared me if that had been the case. But events had transpired so quickly. Could I have simply forgotten what she told me? The last time we spoke, I was preparing to usher my grandchildren out the door after a summer visit. In my haste to get off the phone, had I missed something?

This is what I remembered her saying: "We have a baby. A ten-month-old. Severe scalding. The mother was sent packing. They think she did it. They're from Mississippi. He's been here for weeks and nobody's come to see him. You wanted to volunteer. How about coming to the hospital to sit and hold him when you're in town?"

No longer a question. Here I was. As my eyes drifted upward, I prepared for the worst. Suddenly I remembered something Kanika had told me. "In medical school we're told to keep our eyebrows down and our mouths closed when taking histories or performing physical exams; surprise is never an appropriate response."

At the head of the mammoth bed was a small body. *Focus,* I told myself. You're in a cold, sterile hospital room—surprise is not an appropriate response. Finally, I looked into Baby B's face. Fixed on me, unwavering, unflinching, were eyes as big as cupcakes, velvety milk chocolate, shaded by long lovely lashes, curling like calligraphy.

How brave you are, Baby B, I thought . . . *still able to look upon a human face so boldly.*

CHAPTER 2

The Offering

"Children's talent to endure stems from their ignorance of alternatives."

—*Maya Angelou*

His HEAD WAS wrapped in white bandages, snug like the soft pink and blue skullcaps newborns wore to keep their tender heads warm. Baby B was nine months old. He was admitted to the hospital near death. Kanika said he had mounds of lovely hair before they shaved his head closer than a bare Buddha's. I imagined thick, dark, silky, baby hair floating down onto the operating room floor like burnt offerings from a funeral pyre.

The nurse looked toward me. "Aren't those eyes something else?" she said. "They lock like radar onto anybody who comes through the door until someone else enters. Then they zero in on that person." She stood over him talking, but his eyes held to mine. "I think we got them all, Dr. Bowen." The two of them had finally finished unsnarling the tubes that snaked out from Baby B's nose, chest, hands, and below his waist like the tentacles of some alien sci-fi figure.

"What are all of the tubes for?" I asked.

"A feeding nasal gastric tube and central and arterial lines," my daughter answered. "Do you want to hold him?"

For some reason, her question caught me by surprise. That was, after all, why I was there—to hold him. But it seemed so out of proportion to all that he required. I replied, "Sure," as if she were asking me whether I would like to share a dessert, and I agreed because I knew how much she wanted it.

I moved to the one chair in the room. It was not a chair made for holding a hurt child. It was a hard chair with rigid metal armrests built for sitting up straight, observing, and taking notes. There were no pictures or personal items present that indicated that Baby B had a connection with anybody in the world. I buffered the chair with several pillows and waited for Baby B's deliverance. Kanika and the nurse moved as a unified perfected duo toward me, gripping the IV stand, juggling tubes, and cradling Baby B until he was safely deposited onto the pillow atop my waiting lap. He stared at me. I stared at him. "Hi, Baby B," I said in a cheerful, chirpy bird voice that sounded nothing like mine. The only exposed parts of his body were his chest, shoulders, and lovely face. The rest of him was encased in bandages that secured molded plastic splints on his feet, arms, legs, and hands to keep them from shriveling and twisting.

I held him gingerly, slightly out from me like an offering. He was so quiet. Not a whimper. We all waited and watched. "You can hold him closer, Mom."

"I don't want to hurt him," I replied. I pulled him slightly nearer, but all I could feel were hard angles and the resistance of his small self to this stranger. He and I eyed one another, guardedly. I am a mother times three. Shouldn't I have had a reservoir of sympathies to soothe this child? The comfort words of the past I once used for bruised knees, hurt fingers, and hurt feelings seemed too trivial for this time and place. Kanika and the nurse finished remaking the bed with the antiseptic-treated white hospital sheets worn so soft from washings they felt like silk. They came to stand over us. "Let's see if he'll take a little water," the nurse said. He took a few sucks from the nipple when it touched his lips. He did not reach for the bottle. His eyes remained on mine.

"He hasn't taken any liquids in a while. You did good, Mom."

I wondered how long it had been since he had been held close rather than held down.

CHAPTER 3

Detour

"Life is what happens when you're busy making plans."
—Allen Saunders

FOR A LONG time and quite naively so, I thought my life was set on a predictable trajectory, like a child's dot-to-dot drawing. With little pauses to make sure I was on the right track, I would go from A to B to C until my fairytale picture was complete. I never considered D might stand for *detour.*

On a sweltering July afternoon, I was relaxing with a novel after attending an exercise class when the phone rang. The house was quiet except for the chirping of birds echoing down the fireplace chimney. No television. No radio. Thumps from the air conditioner revved up and shut down. It annoyed me. I liked the quiet. "'I have never met a companion as companionable as solitude,'" wrote Thoreau.

The phone rang.

I peered at the caller ID and saw my daughter's number. Kanika was an intern at the University of Texas Medical Branch (UTMB) at Galveston. I tossed the book aside, grabbed the receiver, and slid down deeper on the recliner, ready to hear tales of human triumphs and tragedies where individuals either survived against all odds or perished despite positive predictions. The hospital is a place of high drama, a microcosm of the best and worst of the human condition. Within its hallowed halls, humanity is forced to bare its soul and suffer the open cotton gown.

I heard the beeps and clicks bouncing from the machines surrounding the nurse's station coming through the receiver. "Hey, sweetie, what's up in the halls of gods?" The quip was a running joke between the two of us based on the book I had given her, a comedic tale about the personal and professional lives of doctors exhibiting the "god complex."

"Hi, Mom. What you doin'?"

She had been on call the previous night and was coming off medical rounds. I was always surprised how alert and upbeat she sounded despite her strenuous schedule. It was clear she loved being a doctor. The first thing she always asked was what I was doing, as if my actions altered in any significant way from day to day. Her days were the ones filled with change. She was the one making life and death decisions doused in the blood of strangers. During our talk, she shared some of the night's highlights and her need to go home and get some sleep, but said she still needed to review lab reports and update patient files.

"We're coming up this weekend," I responded. "I'm going to visit Baby B. How is he doing?" It had been a couple of weeks since I had cradled Baby B in my arms in that stark hospital room and watched as he took small sucks from a bottle.

"About the same. But he needs to get out of here."

"What do you mean?"

"At rounds this morning, the chief of surgery said Baby B is at a turning point. Certain things need to happen before he can leave the hospital."

"Such as?"

"One—he needs to be eating."

"Two—he needs to be out of bed."

"And three—he needs to be held."

She rattled the mandates off in her efficient "list of things to do" demeanor. I pictured her standing there in her white coat, concentrating, checking off each item.

"Well," I said, letting the words drip out, "aren't the nurses supposed to be doing that?"

"They're doing the best they can, but he needs so much more than they can do."

And then she said words that would reverberate back to me again and again.

"Too bad you can't be here."

The words weren't spoken with any malice. She was simply stating a fact. Baby B did need someone to be there for him on an ongoing basis. But I was not that person. He needed more than I could do. I had raised my family without any help from anyone. It was my time now.

*   *   *

Lawrence and I married too young. Had children too young but managed to raise them to responsible adulthood and send them all to college. They graduated and were good, decent tax-paying citizens. They never returned home to "find themselves" or to "save money." And we felt fortunate we had beaten the odds. It was our time now. We enjoyed doing all the things we didn't have time or money for back in the day: traveling, eating out, and playing. We spent our spare time maintaining our mature bodies so that we could keep moving. Earlier that year we had hiked to the bottom of the Grand Canyon with Kanika and our older daughter, Nicole. After returning home, Lawrence and I purchased kayaks and began mapping out Texas lakes and rivers. In short, we were finding nothing empty about the empty nest.

"Yes, it is too bad," I replied, then steered our conversation toward repairs Lawrence would make on Kanika's little bungalow while we were in Galveston. Before hanging up, I promised to bring her some of my homemade mango relish.

From the recliner, I saw a little lizard trapped between the windowpane and screen, scurrying for a way out. The street was deserted and the day was as dry and still as a desert. The only things missing were twirling dust devils and rolling tumbleweeds. In Texas, the spring window slammed shut in mid-May. After that, the dial on the thermometer tipped toward triple digits. Yellow buses had expelled their last charges and rumbled back to the holding pens. School was out, but the suburban streets were empty of children. The neighborhood was on summer lockdown, and so then was my mood. I knew that my bimonthly visits to Baby B were only a modicum of what he needed, but I had felt good about the small part I was playing. Now they seemed as pointless as trying to point the way out to the little lizard.

CHAPTER 4

Good-bye, Byahlia

"The family you come from isn't as important as the family you're going to have."

—*Ring Lardner*

On Monday, July 18, 2005, at approximately 10 p.m., Baby B was rushed by ambulance from a housing project in Byhalia, Mississippi, to the emergency room of Le Bonheur Children's Medical Center in Memphis, Tennessee. He was admitted with second- and third-degree scald burns, full thickness to over 65 percent of his body. Third-degree or full-thickness burns involve destruction of the entire dermis, leaving only subcutaneous tissue exposed. It is characterized by lack of sensation in the burned skin, a leathery texture, and destroyed blood vessels. The 65 percent coverage began at his nipple line, extended downward to his abdomen, and included his forearms, hands, lower buttocks, legs, and feet. Records document, "He was brought in extremis," meaning near death. In seven days if he survived, he would turn ten months old.

He was intubated and a nasogastric tube was inserted.

Intravenous lines carried saline solution to prevent his body
from going into shock and morphine to mute the screaming
pain. Silvadene cream was applied to control infection. After
being stabilized in emergency, Baby B was taken to the intensive
care unit.

Because of the circumstances surrounding his injuries,
authorities suspected neglect at the very least. On Tuesday about
four in the morning Faye, the biological mother, was interviewed
by a hospital employee using a Peds Psychosocial Assessment
intake form. Possible neglect was listed under assessment type.
The intake form consisted of categories listing family history
and constellation and statements by Faye. Even if her version
of the events was to be believed, it showed a shocking disregard
for even a minute amount of safety regarding her children.

Faye stated that on Monday night at about 9 p.m., she ran
bath water for Baby B and his two-year-old brother and placed
both in the tub. She said that she went to take out the garbage,
leaving both boys alone in the tub of water.

It was the middle of July. At 9 p.m., light was beginning to
fade. School was out for the summer, and outside the children
were running around in circles. The teenage boys were circling
the basketball hoops, and the teenage girls were circling the
boys. Adults were outside as well, putting off going back into
their hot apartments.

In order to carry her garbage to the disposal site, Faye had
to walk at least thirty to forty feet from her apartment. She
did not report that she encountered any of her neighbors as
she was leaving or returning to her apartment. She stated that
when she finally reentered her apartment, she did not go to the
bathroom to check on the boys. Instead, she said she went to
another room to get their bedclothes. She stated she heard the
two-year-old turn on the water and shouted at him to turn it off.
She said that when she finally went into the bathroom she saw

Baby B's two-year-old brother standing behind him and Baby B sitting under the faucet of running hot water. She stated Baby B was not crying or screaming at any time and that his two-year-old brother was not injured, although he was standing in the same tub of scalding water. Brown flecks (detached skin) were floating in the water.

The interviewer took less than ten minutes to get a verbal statement from the birth mother and enter a six-line clinical finding on the assessment form in the computer, concluding with, "Mother was tearful and upset in describing what happened to the patient. Mother was concerned about patient's health and well-being."

After reading the report, the admitting doctor insisted the interviewer go back and attach the following: "Dr. O reported that the injuries do not fit the explanation given."

Faye would later give three different versions of the same story, including one version in which she indicated someone else might have been present and might have been responsible. Who was responsible for sorting all that out now that he was about to be transported to another state? Saving his life took precedence over everything else. Faye took advantage of this interval to hide in plain sight from the authorities.

* * *

Le Bonheur hospital did not have a specialty burn unit. It functioned as the region's primary level 1 pediatric trauma center. The medical center had more than five hundred medical staff members representing forty-five pediatric specialties. The pediatric residency program was affiliated with the University of Tennessee Health Science Center. The children's hospital primarily served children from ninety-five counties and six states including Tennessee, Mississippi, Alabama, and Arkansas. It had to be ready for anything.

In ICU, doctors and nurses readied the room and adjusted the temperature to a sweltering ninety degrees. Baby B could have easily become hypothermic due to the massive areas of missing skin. In the first step in the process of helping his body to repair itself, more skin would be removed. A procedure called the Parkland formula for fluid resuscitation in major burns involving infants and young children would be initiated. The next morning he would be evacuated by PediFlite helicopter to the specialty burn hospital for children in Texas. But that night he would spend sedated, encircled in warmth.

CHAPTER 5

Touchdown in Texas

"Leaving behind nights of terror and fear I rise . . ."
—*Maya Angelou*

EARLY TUESDAY MORNING on July 19, 2005, Baby B was taken aboard a fixed-wing aircraft for transport to Shriners Burn Hospital for Children in Galveston, Texas.

What was on the minds of the PediFlite crew as they surrounded Baby B, lifting him up and away from the nightmare? Even as veterans of tragedies involving children, at least one of them must have been on the brink of tears. Perhaps Baby B was conscious enough to briefly open his soft brown eyes and peer out from underneath his massive mound of dark, curly hair. I bet that drew a smile from someone. No emotion was wasted on pity. Pity should be reserved for those who have surrendered hope, for those without family or friends or love in their life. It should be reserved for those who cannot rise up spiritually or physically, to fight back.

You only fight if you hold the hope of winning. Baby B never stopped fighting for his life. He fought for it the night the ambulance arrived; he fought for it in the emergency room at Le Bonheur; he fought for it in days and weeks of hospitalization and rehabilitation at Shriners. As he fought to survive and grow stronger, he drew to him an ever-expanding circle of people who surrounded him with loving care. Finally, when he was strong enough to leave the hospital, a family came to carry him into their hearts.

* * *

Operators notified Shriners Hospital that the plane had landed, and the ambulance was in route. The burn team was already assembling on the second floor of ICU. Like any team trained to win, each member of the burn brigade knew his or her position and executed each move with skill and precision. The team dressed in the loose structure of surgical scrubs. The flexible garb matched the temperaments of the team. Rigidity was a structure that would snap under the weight of the volitant environment of the burn unit. The faded blue or green tops and pants could easily be discarded as the surgeons traipsed in and out of the operating room. The surgeons rarely wore white coats. No stethoscopes dangled down their chests. Burn patients require lots of surgeries; it is the rule rather than the exception. There is no time to shed extra gear.

Once Baby B was placed in bed in ICU, he was hooked up to tubes linked to machines that delivered meds and recorded life signs. Clear-liquid bottles suspended from pole hooks delivered a flood of fluids. The layers of wrappings encasing his body were examined for signs of leakage or infection. Later that evening, he was given additional pain medication and taken to the tub room, where he was soaked in the wrappings until they and the dead skin were loosened enough to be sloughed off. His flesh was scrutinized and scrubbed and rewrapped. The medication did not vanquish the pain.

CHAPTER 6

Shriners

*"I love people who harness themselves, an ox to a heavy
cart, who pull like water buffalo,
with massive patience,
who strain in the mud and muck to move things forward,
who do what has to be done, again and again."*

—*Marge Piercy*

SHRINERS BURN HOSPITAL for Children in Galveston
opened in 1966, but its island relationship can be traced
back to 1963, when it opened a seven-bed ward in the
John Sealy Hospital. The unassuming seven-story beige brick
and mortar building sits on the corner of 8th and Market Street.
It is a total burn care treatment facility, specializing in the care
of all types of burns: chemical, fire, scalding, and microwave.

Children from all over the world are treated there without
regard to socio-economic status. The cost of caring for burn
injuries is completely covered from the time of acute injury
through rehabilitation and individual reconstructive needs
until age eighteen. This is truly amazing when you calculate the
tremendous number of dollars it takes to care for one burned

child. More importantly, parents and caretakers are not saddled with the added stress of astronomical medical bills. There is a motto that welcomes parents as they enter the revolving doors of the hospital: *Once a Shriners child, always a Shriners child.* Shriners Hospital is a successful philanthropic effort of epic proportions by the Shriners of North America.

Directly across the street stands John Sealy Hospital, a University of Texas Medical Branch affiliate and a strategic partner with Shriners in comprehensive burn care. Medical students, residents, interns, and staff doctors rotate between the two, each bringing their own brand of expertise and experience. Sealy has its own adult burn unit and is the only state-owned and -operated multi-disciplinary hospital in Texas. Together this trinity—Shriners, UTMB, and Sealy—form a titanic team in the advancement of burn treatment. If a child you love is ever forced to crawl through hell, pray this team is waiting on the other side.

Galveston Island

The Galveston economy is driven by tourism. Vacationers from the surrounding metropolitan cities of Houston, Austin, and Dallas and smaller communities in between are drawn to Galveston Island because they can access it easily for a weekend getaway via the expressways. The billboards sprouting up along the highway grow taller and wider every year, shouting the best island food and hotel accommodations, but not necessarily the natural resources. "If you're looking for blue waters and pristine beaches, we don't have them," said a representative of tourism after a barrage of complaints about the murky waters, the washed-up seaweed, and the washed-out beach. "But we do have blue skies, sunshine, and the seawall."

The island has a small town atmosphere with an eclectic

assemblage of residents. Like the hospital where the janitor and cafeteria server work in close proximity to the doctor and the nurse, the same dynamic exists in the residential neighborhoods of Galveston's core community. Professionals reside on the same tree-lined streets as service workers and small business owners. During peak summer seasons, people from all walks of life form a colorful promenade along the seawall. Families with teenagers and toddlers in tow lug ice chests up and down Seawall Boulevard looking for the perfect patch of sand to stake their claim to paradise. Then there are the daredevils—bikers, surfers, wanderers—who descend upon what they have come to cherish for its reputation as a working class summer retreat. Some call it "The Little Big Easy." They all ride in on a giant wave of sun worship and salt air at the beginning of summer and wash out at the end of the season, sunburned and satisfied.

Some vacationers venture beyond Seawall Boulevard to a place where shopping replaces sunbathing. The nostalgic city center is known as The Strand. Located about five miles from the main drag of the seawall, The Strand is the pride of Galveston. Positioned in an upscale historic district, it boasts an expansive array of expensive shops housed in Victorian buildings. Horse-drawn carriages rolling along brick-paved streets transport people back in time. Unique corner museums, intimate little restaurants, and sidewalk dining dominate the area.

However, few visitors will ever venture into the most exciting, drama-driven district on this island, because what takes place there has little to do with pleasure or fun. It covers more than eight busy blocks, but there are no billboards proclaiming its greatness. It's not on the list of tourist attractions. But if a vacation takes an unexpected turn toward a medical emergency, this is the place where the lighthouse always shines. It is the medical complex containing John Sealy Hospital and Shriners Burn Hospital for Children.

Surrounding the hospitals is a conglomerate of facilities that support the medical community: medical libraries, laboratories, research and rehabilitation centers. Fast food restaurants and small gourmet sandwich shops are within walking distance. The medical establishment is the largest employer of Galveston residents and the surrounding communities.

A few miles from this sprawling medical complex are some desolate blocks that run parallel to railroad tracks, where residents of a public housing project can look across and see the huge cruise ships that are docked, waiting to depart on tropical cruises. The projects, like the people who inhabit them, remain largely invisible to tourists and residents alike.

The island has had more than its own share of close calls. On September 8, 1900, a massive hurricane made landfall at Galveston. The hurricane would rate a Category 4 on today's hurricane scale, as winds topped 150 miles per hour and a storm surge was estimated at thirteen to eighteen feet. Property damage and six thousand lives lost in this storm led to the construction in 1902 of a seventeen-foot-high concrete seawall that has been expanded to 10.4 miles along the most populated section of the Gulf. This is the same seawall enjoyed by thousands each year as they walk, run, skate, bike, or fly kites that soar above it all.

The threat of impending hurricanes is a seasonal reality on the Gulf Coast. However, the Galveston seawall and early warning and evacuation procedures have served to greatly reduce the loss of life and property. Nevertheless, precautions can only reduce, never eliminate, destruction caused by natural disasters.

Evacuation would become a continuing theme in the life of Baby B as he fled danger. And two more horrendous hurricanes would threaten the very existence of Galveston Island.

CHAPTER 7

It Takes a Village

"You can't help someone get up a hill without getting closer yourself."

—*H. Norman Schwarzkopf*

YEARS BEFORE KANIKA's birth, I worked as a coordinator at Veterans Hospitals in California and Oklahoma. I loved my job inside the always-fluid medical environment. At the end of the day, I felt I had accomplished something significant. I am proud that my daughter belongs to a profession that saves lives. She said she had always known she wanted to be a doctor. Because of the way she spent her school years, taking the hard sciences, graduating a year early from high school, and finishing medical school at age twenty-four, I don't doubt that. She has always been focused, stubborn, and single-minded. She is also compassionate, loyal, and loving, so her dedication to her profession comes as no surprise.

After Kanika became a medical student at UTMB, my husband and I began making regular visits to that Gulf community. Soon tourist attractions lost their luster and beachcombing forays onto the gritty Galveston beach no longer yielded any surprises for me. It was then that I told Kanika I wanted to volunteer a few hours at Shriners on the weekends when I was in Galveston. It seemed like a perfect way to contribute and connect with the community she served. Perhaps she and I would meet for lunch in the cafeteria occasionally. "But I don't want to waste my time," I had said. "I don't want to be one of those little old ladies in the pink uniforms who smile and sit. I have skills, and I have a brain. I want something specific; I want to help somebody."

Lawrence and I usually left Austin for the island on Fridays. On Saturday afternoons I visited Baby B. I watched him while he slept, sang to him when he was agitated, and held him when he could tolerate touch. Most of the time he was too sedated and too traumatized to sense my presence. Those times, I could only sit beside his bed and speak softly to him through the rails. There was an army of hospital staff in and out of his room. I was only one more in a long line of strangers trailing in and out. I considered myself a temporary stand-in rather than a long-term solution. The one person whom he might have recognized, for better or worse, was Faye. But she had been banished from Shriners and sent back to Mississippi, branded as a suspect in the scalding. Doctors made the determination that it was impossible for Baby B to have sustained injuries the way in which she described the events, and "that and her lack of genuine emotion or concern during her times at the hospital" were red alerts. She had vanished from the hospital several times when Baby B was in the midst of critical surgeries.

Her banishment meant that I was spared the awkwardness of encountering her during my visits. What would have been our reaction to one another if I had walked into Baby B's room, and there she was? It would be years before she and I would lock eyes from where she sat in the defendant's chair of a Mississippi courthouse and I sat in the witness seat.

Other family members existed. I was optimistic that someone

would arrive at the eleventh hour. Surely once it became known that Baby B was all alone in a hospital hundreds of miles from home, a family member would come forth. At the same time, I had no Hallmark card expectations. In past years, I had served as a court-appointed special advocate (CASA) volunteer for foster children. I was well aware of the thousands of children residing in foster homes because the people we assume would step up to the plate and go to bat for their children so often do not. Still, in my most optimistic moments I saw some representative of the "it takes a village to raise a child" crowd rushing in to assume responsibility, turning their mantra into a reality. I never imagined I would be the one whom I was seeking.

CHAPTER 8

A Heavy Burden

"Children begin by loving their parents; as they grow older, they judge them; sometimes they forgive them."

—Oscar Wilde

I T WAS JULY and I was well into my summer activity schedule in Austin. A creature of habit, I found comfort in an orderly, predictable life. I had grown up in a chaotic household with an alcoholic father and a chronically depressed mother. Somehow they managed to get through the week, teetering on a tightrope of normalcy balanced by an array of passive-aggressive slights and swipes at one another. But by the time Friday arrived, that tightrope had stretched to a snapping point and all of that pent-up animosity and alienation sent them thrashing through the house. Whatever disappointments or demons my father had simmering during the week reached the boiling point when he poured his first Friday drink. He was movie star handsome with a charming smile and engaging personality. Whenever I heard someone say ". . . but he seemed like such a nice guy" after the "nice guy" had committed some brutal act, I knew exactly what kind of person they were describing.

Sometimes when he beat her, I hid and dialed "0" and laid the phone down, hoping the operator would hear my mother's screams. One night two police officers actually came. When my father heard the sirens, he ran into the schoolyard behind our house. My mother hated the siren broadcasting her plight to the neighbors more than being beaten. "What happens in the family stays in the family."

The police strolled through the house past the wreckage to the backyard. My brother and I stood behind my mother, watching the police question her: "Which way did he go, ma'am?"

"I don't know. That way, I think." She pointed in the opposite direction that he had run.

"No, Mommy," I began, "he went. . . ." I raised my hand. She grabbed it, crushing it in her grip as I looked up into her bruised, battered face.

"She didn't see anything; she doesn't know what she's talking about," my mother shot back.

The policemen turned and retraced their steps. At the front door, one paused. "You might want to tell your kids to stop playing with the phone, ma'am. We don't want to have to come back here again."

My mother peeked from behind the curtain and watched them leave. She turned to me and bent down, pressing her mouth next to my ear, squeezing both of my cheeks hard with her hand, and whispered, "Never, ever tell them where your father is."

Sometimes my parents would separate my brother and me like felons, taking each of us to a different room. "Who do you want to live with, if we get a divorce?" My father didn't know that my mother had already warned my brother and me that if either of us said we wanted to live with him, we would never see her again. "I stay for you," she told us. "So you can have a father." It was a heavy burden to chain to a child.

My father always responded the same way when we said without hesitation that we wanted to stay with our mother. He cried. Triumphant, my mother gathered us around him and patted his shoulder like a toddler. "Tell your father you love him," she purred. I was more bewildered by his tears than disturbed because those were the only times that I considered it a possibility he might actually love my brother and me. I hated my father for his brutality and my mother for bowing to it. Still, I loved them.

My mother was a beautiful, smart woman, but she was as addicted to my father as he was to the bottle. Saddled with her own emotional extremes, she added the extra weight of being my father's enabler. Ever watchful, she placated him—until she couldn't. Except for the fact that the tempest always arrived on a Friday, the eruptions were unpredictable, coming out of nowhere, like a hurricane. Rumbles of trouble on the horizon surfaced around twilight. But the full force of the night storm and its destructive aftermath were always a surprise. Together, their relationship was "The back of the hand to everything," as written in Mary Oliver's poem, "Hurricane."

When my brother and I came out of our hiding places after my parents had finally retreated to their room, we took furtive steps through the house, in the eerie silence, sad surveyors of the wrecked surroundings. Chairs and tables were overturned, mirrors cracked, doors ripped off cabinets, their contents pitched. The refrigerator door hung open with its bright beam pouring out, spotlighting scattered piles of tossed food. The floor was splashed with colorful palettes of jelly, juice, soups, and sauces, mimicking some mad artist's abstract painting.

The next morning, my parents would emerge from their room, gentle and giving toward one another, speaking in soft whispers. Had it not been for the mess in the kitchen, I might have convinced myself I had dreamt the previous night. I don't need a therapist to help me determine where my craving for consistency and calm originates.

CHAPTER 9

Holding Hope, Gripping Grief

"The first question which the priest and the Levite asked was: 'If I stop to help this man, what will happen to me?' But . . . the good Samaritan reversed the question: 'If I do not stop to help this man, what will happen to him?'"

—Bible, Luke 10:30-37

THROUGH JULY AND into August my husband and I traveled to Galveston every other weekend. The weeks flew by; I kept a suitcase packed. I continued visiting Baby B at Shriners. I had no illusions that I made any great impact on his recovery. However, the thought of not going seemed cowardly and selfish. Even if I replaced those few hours I had committed to him with something else, he would have remained with me in the midst of it.

On Saturday afternoons I rode the elevator to the second floor, and said hello to the nurses at the station who recognized me as "Dr. Bowen's mother." I always performed the same ritual, pulling on gown and gloves before entering his room. The human skin provides perfect protection against invading germs. When it is missing, as it was with Baby B, the body becomes a magnet for infection.

Sometimes he was asleep when I arrived and remained so until I left. I never tried to wake him, thinking he might be sedated or that he needed sleep more than he needed me. During those times, I felt utterly useless. I watched the nurses come and go, take vital signs, check machines, and adjust tubes. They acknowledged me with a nod or a smile, but they never discussed Baby B's care or condition with me. I had no legal standing, and was therefore not entitled to know any more than I could observe for myself.

Under different circumstances, I would not have hesitated to pitch in and do the normal things a mother would do for a child in the hospital, but I feared violating some protocol—if one existed. Indeed, I may have been the first volunteer (if that was how I was regarded) allowed because volunteers were rarely permitted on the children's unit of a hospital. More importantly, nonessential pedestrian traffic would have put children on the burn unit at an increased risk of infection. But because Baby B had no other visitors, my positive presence in his life outweighed any negative.

If Baby B happened to be awake, his eyes would follow my every move, although he never uttered a sound. I played soft baby lullabies for him from a small CD player on a counter next to his bed. Sometimes I read him poems or nursery rhymes from books I had brought with me. I massaged the parts of him that were not covered with wrapping in small, circular movements with my finger.

A large television loomed from the ceiling at the foot of the bed. I never turned it on. My interpretation of hell was to be incapacitated, unable to speak or move, chained to a television, with a sitcom's laugh track blaring. As it was, the dark face of the television held only the stillness and sterility of the room.

* * *

When I was in Austin, Kanika and I called each other frequently with typical mother and daughter banter. I never tired of hearing tales from the dark side of medical school. Of course, we never ended a call without her filling me in on Baby B's progress, or the lack thereof. She was considerate enough not to burden me with details of the day-to-day suffering he endured.

Once I became a regular visitor to Shriners, I recognized surgeons immediately. Their hair was matted, their faces were ashen, and their view seemed to be concentrated in the few feet just ahead of them. They looked as if they had just rolled out of bed. The truth is many times they never made it home to their own beds. When on call, they existed on as little as four hours of sleep a night. Surgery was a round-the-clock activity, either emergency or scheduled. When they were able to sleep, they went to spare quarters in a single room in the hospital, where they could be found quickly and roused.

As mid-August approached, Dr. H, the chief of surgery, grew increasingly impatient with the failure of social services to find someone willing to accept responsibility for Baby B's care after discharge. I was surprised to discover that this was the same doctor I occasionally encountered walking down the corridors or waiting in front of elevators. On those occasions, he would nod at me or remark, "It's a hot one today," or "Back again?"

"I don't think he knows I'm your mother," I smiled.

"He knows," Kanika replied.

At over six feet tall, Dr. H was accustomed to looming over others. With gray hair and horn-rimmed glasses, he exuded a casualness that contradicted the life and death decisions he made every day. He told others that his part was to make decisions that took death out of the equation. He was a fervent fighter for the life of his patients. He wanted to save burned children's lives—period. He believed quality of life issues occurred post-surgery and were to be accepted and dealt with on that basis, not debated. He knew that not everyone agreed with his philosophy, but he was steadfast in his stance.

Every morning except weekends, the entire medical team (psychologist, social worker, physical therapists, nurses, medical students, and doctors) spearheaded by Dr. H made grand rounds on the second floor, a twelve-bed unit equipped to treat children in various states of transition from being newly burned to burn rehabilitation status.

One morning I watched and listened as the team moved in unison, weaving in and out of each room. Parents waited anxiously at the doorway of their child's room, pacing in and out, peering up and down the corridor, holding hope in one hand, gripping grief in the other. The parents prayed that whatever news the doctors delivered that morning would be better than the day before. They imagined the doctor saying, "Yes, the infection is gone," or "No, those scars won't be permanent," or "Sure, we can fix that." Each new day brought enough hope to sustain until the next day.

Finally, it was Baby B's turn. No one waited or hoped at his door.

The procession poured through the doorway. Crowding in, everyone shuffled into position, coming shoulder to shoulder around the bed. The stark fluorescent lights magnified the metal bed railings, the bleached white sheets, the doctors' white coats. Baby B's little body took up a fraction of the bed, as still and silent as a baby bird in an elaborate nest.

Dr. H instructed a medical student to give a brief history. Protocols were discussed, lab results reported, and medications scrutinized. He canvassed the team for input and answers.

He had a caustic sense of humor, and anyone who voiced an opinion without a rational reason and factual basis was likely to be the recipient of his cutting wit. The next goal for Baby B: discharge from the hospital to a home where he could continue rehabilitation and prescribed healing therapies. Dr. H glared at the social worker. An awkward silence ensued. He held up his hand and counted off on his fingers, speaking as if he were talking to a recalcitrant child. "Three things need to happen," he stated. "One, he needs to be out of bed; two, he needs to be moving more; three, he needs to be eating more. That can't happen here. Find some place it can."

More than thirty days had passed since Baby B's admission to Shriners in July. Though he had survived and passed the critical period, he was not getting the kind of stimulation needed to leapfrog him to the next crucial stage. The lack of intimate physical contact and loving emotional interaction added a burden to both his physical and mental health. His hospital room was a sensory assault chamber. Hospital personnel were in and out of his room at all hours of the day and night, lights on, lights off, bed changes and dressing changes, needle pricks, physical therapy. It was an ongoing deluge of aching activity. A lingering worry was that the longer he remained in the hospital, the greater the chance of his contracting an opportunistic infection.

Baby B was in a holding pattern without an end date. With the exception of Kanika and me, he had no other visitors. No hand caressed his soft baby face. No one was waiting to comfort and calm him after he was returned by gurney from the daily phalanx of painful procedures. No soothing voice smothered night terrors. He was receiving the best medical care in the world—activity surrounded him constantly—yet he was utterly alone.

The social worker had already contacted various family

members in an effort to convince someone to come to Shriners for a brief visit or extended stay to help with Baby B's recovery: free room and board available through Ronald McDonald House only a few blocks from the hospital, free transportation from Mississippi to Texas and multiple other incentives in an effort to encourage family participation. She had contacted state social service agencies both in Baby B's home state of Mississippi and in Texas for help in finding a foster family, but both states already had thousands of healthy children in desperate need of foster homes. Social workers were camping out overnight in state offices with children because they could not find adequate foster homes. Child advocacy groups were filing lawsuits to stop that practice. No one wanted to take on a case as complicated as Baby B's because of the intensive oversight it required and the complicated legal issues surrounding trans-state foster care.

Furthermore, there was always an acute shortage of therapeutic foster families. Potential caretakers had to be certified as a therapeutic home by the state, which in most cases required a college degree or minimum amount of medical training. Baby B's catastrophic injuries would require a foster family committed to his care twenty-four hours a day, seven days a week. They would have to be trained in burn care. They would have to take Baby B to Shriners one or more times a day for treatments and therapies. They would have to maintain a daily record of intake and output regarding food, liquids, and medication. In addition, they would have to fill out multiple monthly social service reports.

Each morning on medical rounds with increased agitation, Dr. H hurled the same question at the social worker. "Have you found a place for him yet?"

Finally in desperation, the social worker turned to a Galveston private foster care agency. Because of high caseloads, backlogs, and employee turnovers, the Texas Department of Health and

Human Services had just started an experimental program whereby it contracted with private agencies to find families and supervise foster care. Nonetheless, by mid-August, both the social worker and the private foster agency had failed to find a family willing to take on such an enormous responsibility. Kanika grew increasingly concerned as she watched Baby B linger in the hospital day after day and night after night. We talked about the awful quagmire in which he was stuck, sinking slowly not from lack of medical care, but from lack of the basic human closeness and contact essential to his very survival. I hung up the phone and closed my eyes, and saw Baby B's eyes, wide and waiting. Soon the sun would go down, and he would spend another night alone. Tomorrow the sun would rise, and he would face another day alone.

The image would not leave me. When I least expected it, he would materialize, wide-eyed and waiting. Why couldn't I do more for him? Why shouldn't I? I contemplated the costs of giving up a few months of my life and the impact those months might have on Baby B's entire life. The summer was ending. Once my grandchildren started school in a few weeks, I would not see them again until my son brought them back for Thanksgiving.

My husband did not require my constant presence. Of course he would miss me, but he would stay busy and time would pass quickly. Besides, he loved Galveston. He would have an excuse to go more often if I were there. Nicole lived nearby and was busy working and pursuing her master's degree in education. She and I talked regularly on the phone, but we could still do that if I were in Galveston. I was sure she would support her sister's and my decision, given her love of children.

It dawned on me—like when you're daydreaming and driving and suddenly realize that you've driven past your destination—I had gone beyond the point where my family was dependent on me.

CHAPTER 10

A Matter of Months

"We must be willing to get rid of the life we planned so as to have the life that is waiting for us."
　　　　　　　　　　　　　　　　　—*Joseph Campbell*

I CALLED KANIKA a few days later. "Maybe," I said, "just to get Baby B out of the hospital . . . I could come up for a little while . . . you know, just until they find someone else and—"

"Oh Mom, that would be great!"

"Wait, wait. I'd have to talk it over with your dad first." Something shifted in my stomach. "And we're just talking for a few weeks, right? They should be able to find somebody by then, shouldn't they?"

"Oh yeah," she replied. "I'll make sure they know that . . . you know . . . we're just doing this to get him out of the hospital and they have to find somebody."

"Okay then. You'll let me know what they say?"

"Yeah, yeah. I'll start working on it right away. Bye, Mom. Love you."

I continued to hold the phone in my hand until the

recording—"hang up and try again." Well, it probably wouldn't happen anyway. This wasn't the way things were done. Hospitals did not turn over sick babies to total strangers, even well-meaning ones. I put off talking with Lawrence. No need opening up a can of worms about something that probably would not happen.

* * *

Kanika called the following week. "It's all been arranged," she said.

I had just returned from my three-mile walk and opened the door to the ringing phone. Lawrence and I had reserved a room at the Big Bend National Park Lodge for a hiking weekend in a few months, and I wanted to be in shape so I could keep up without huffing and puffing. My endorphins had me euphoric; it took a moment for her words to sink in. "What?"

"For Baby B," said Kanika

"That fast," I said.

"Yeah," she said, "I guess they wanted to move fast before we changed our minds, although it's not like they have a choice. So I'm going to take off next week and you . . ."

"Wait a minute," I said. "What do you mean you're going to take off? You're a resident. You can't just take off!" My daughter could be as impulsive as me. But she had a lot more to lose.

"No, no, no. Listen." she said. "Let me back up."

I pressed my lips together, forcing myself to stay silent. "Go ahead."

"We made rounds this morning as usual. So they started that old one-step, two-step dance about what to do with Baby B."

"They? Who's they?" I jabbed.

"Dr. H and the social worker. Dr. H asked her, 'Have you found someone to take him?' And she said, 'No, not yet.' I thought to myself, what a surprise. That's when I said . . . I'd take him. You should have been there, Mom. The room got as quiet as a tomb."

"I bet," I said. I envisioned everyone in the room staring at her in disbelief, especially the other residents. Surgical residencies were fiercely competitive—getting in and staying on a medical team. They must have thought her insane. "Then what?"

"Dr. H looked at me and said, 'And how are you going to manage that?'"

"And you said?"

"I told him that I had a week's vacation, and I would use it to take care of Baby B, and my mother would come down and take care of him until they could find someone."

My mind raced to keep up with what she was telling me. "And did they happen to say when that might be?" I asked, my voice heavy on the *be*.

"The social worker said she thought they could find someone by the time Baby B's wounds closed around October," replied Kanika.

October. That meant I would be back home for the holidays. "So, just until October," I said. "Anything else?"

"Nope. He told the social worker to make it happen. And then you know what Dr. H said to me, Mom?"

"What?"

"'He's yours,'" she replied.

"Yours?" I repeated.

"Yeah, you know, temporarily," she said. "Isn't it great?" Her voice rose the way it did when she was a little girl and excited. I rarely heard that kind of enthusiasm in my day-to-day dealings with people. It was as if people hadn't the energy to force a smile. Everywhere I went people seemed solemn, joyless, shut off, even angry.

"You did say October, right?"

"Yep," she replied.

"All right," I said. "I should be able to handle that."

"So I'm taking off next week. Can you come down the week after?" she asked.

"I think so," I stammered, my mind racing. "You know I have to talk to your dad. He has to agree."

"Yeah, I know. I know," she replied. "But he knows that you go to see Baby B when you guys are down here."

"Yes, Kanika," I said, "but he doesn't know that you and I are talking about *this*. My spending a few hours at the hospital when we're visiting you and spending a few months in Galveston alone aren't exactly equivalent."

"You won't be alone," she said. "You'll be with Baby B and me."

Kanika had felt deeply for Baby B since the day she saw him. That was why it didn't surprise me that, given the circumstances that confronted her, she broke ranks, stepped forward, and gathered his life into her hands. What did surprise me was how the months would roll over like waves and render time irrelevant. There would come a point when time would simply stand still.

CHAPTER 11

A Dream Come True

"It is not what you collect in life that matters; it is not the things we have but what we have shared that tells the kind of life you've lived."

—*Anonymous*

L AWRENCE AND I had no idea that Kanika would become a medical student on UTMB-Galveston when we began going to the island for weekend getaways while she was still an undergraduate at Texas A&M. We went to Galveston for the same reasons thousands of other vacationers flocked there—the convenient location and the seawall. We visited her often in Galveston at her small, sparse above-garage apartment that overlooked a courtyard of overgrown oleanders and stunted palm trees with spiky fronds whipped by the island winds. Thorny cockleburs layered the pathway to the apartment, clinging to our clothes, hair, and shoes like leeches.

Her postage stamp-size kitchen window provided a telescopic view down into the weed-choked sandpit backyard of the shotgun house next door (so named because it was said that you could shoot a bullet through the front door and it would travel in a direct path through the back door). Children and a variety of house pets wandered in and out of the open back door of the house to sit or scratch and dig around in the coarse sand or simply to urinate in the yard. At night bright light poured out from inside the house through the windows as a parade of figures moved back and forth between chairs and cots, past boxes piled against the walls. The house vibrated with activity. Each time we visited Kanika, it seemed to be a different group of people inhabiting the house, as if their moving in and out was synchronized with our arrival and departure.

Kanika's landlord, a cantankerous old guy with hair and eyes as gray as a dusty rock, was a dictator. He insisted that tenants keep their windows closed against the sweet sea breezes. "The salt air will ruin my appliances," he grumbled. He often sat in his car and watched the comings and goings of tenants and visitors and complained if some small infraction occurred, such as a beach towel being left on the balcony. When he posted a "No Trespassing" sign, he and his neighbor got into a fistfight over property boundaries. Worse, he had taken to entering my daughter's apartment when she was not there, supposedly to make repairs. Once, he almost walked in on her while she was in the shower.

"Maybe you should look for another place," I urged.

"I don't have time, and besides this place is perfect," she replied. "It's close to the hospital and the beach. It'll be okay, Mom. I sent him a letter and told him that he can't legally come in here without notifying me first."

One Saturday morning in the fall of 2003, I borrowed Kanika's bicycle to ride along the seawall. On my return, I passed the front of the shotgun house. A man emerged through the doorway, dressed from head to toe in protective garb. A plastic cap covered his head, a handkerchief was tied around his nose and mouth, and goggles covered his eyes. A plastic apron ran from his shoulders to his boots, and industrial-type gloves stretched from his hands up to his elbows. Bulging black bags dangled from each hand. A white van, double doors thrown wide open, was parked at the curb.

I made a U-turn and stopped my bike behind the van. I watched him heave the last bag into the van. "Hi," I said. "My daughter lives in the upstairs apartment in the back. Looks like somebody left you a pretty big mess." He stopped working and removed one glove and reached up and pulled the handkerchief covering his mouth and nose down around his neck.

"Yeah, renters," he snarled. "I own the place. I don't know how human beings live like that . . . trash all over the place. Holes in the walls. And the smell . . ."

Mmm-hmm, that's what slum landlords always say, I thought. "Seems like a lot of people moving in and out. They never seem to stay very long," I said.

"Just long enough to trash the place," he said, crossing his arms and glancing at the house.

"Have you ever considered selling it?" I asked, surprising myself.

"To tell you the truth, it's crossed my mind," he said. "It's hard to let it go, though. I bought the lot first. Then found the house for a steal; it's a relic from the 1900s. Had it moved here. Fixed it up, thinking me and my wife would use it weekends. We live in Houston, but she stopped wantin' to come so I started renting it out. Been nothin' but trouble ever since."

"Well, it gets a little crowded in my daughter's tiny place. If you do decide to sell, would you contact us first? You wouldn't have to bother with a real estate agent and the commission thing."

We exchanged names and numbers. The following week

my husband called him with an offer. By the time we returned to Galveston, we were the proud owners of a two-bedroom, one-bath Texas shotgun house, located one block from the Gulf of Mexico. I had always loved the ocean and dreamed of having a little house near the sea. Ironically, it had become a reality.

Lawrence and I spent our weekends over the next several months hauling away trash the landlord had abandoned after selling us his albatross. Neighbors watched as exterminators erected a billowing green circus tent around the house, trapping termites and other vermin in a noxious chemical cloud. Then we hired plumbers, electricians, and carpenters to make it livable. The rest of it—plastering holes in the wall, painting, replacing fixtures—we did ourselves. Once the house was ready, we rescued Kanika from the evil landlord. She lived in it through the initial stage of her medical training, and we were happy to stay there when we visited.

* * *

As I prepared dinner that evening, I rehearsed in my mind the best way to tell my husband about how our lives might change in the coming months. Lawrence was not a big champion of change, but if I could convince him that my spending the next few months in Galveston would be a temporary detour in our lives in order to help find a permanent solution for Baby B, he would be more apt to agree. I glanced at the clock. I could literally set it according to the time he left for work and returned home. He was as predictable and dependable as a fine-tuned timepiece.

It was our evening to have dinner in the dining room rather than the breakfast area. It was something I had suggested that we do once in a while. "Sure, if you want to," he had replied, not asking why.

For the most part I enjoyed our empty nest, but the empty seats at dinner after decades of facetious family dinners with our children was an unexpected void. The absence of competing voices came with an unwelcome deafness. It was like sitting down at a game table and wondering when the other players were going to arrive. The setting reminded me of how our lives constantly shifted with or without our consent.

"So how was your day?" I asked. We were halfway through our meal.

"Oh, you know," he mumbled, without looking up. "Spent all day in meetings, worked on a couple of projects. This is good," he said as he took aim with his fork at the supermarket rotisserie chicken.

"Thanks," I said. "That's what comes from slaving over a hot stove all day." My response had become a ready joke between us in recognition of the diminishing time I spent in the kitchen. Lucky for me, he was not a picky eater.

"Are we going down to Galveston next weekend?" he asked. I took a long, slow drink of water as I tried to think of an answer to his question that would encapsulate everything that our daughter and I had discussed regarding Baby B. Lawrence looked up when I didn't respond to his question. "Did you hear me?" he asked.

"Yes, I heard you," I replied. "You want to know if we're going to Galveston next weekend."

"Well?" He looked slightly irritated. "I need to go ahead and schedule Friday off if we want to get an early start."

Lawrence looked forward to our Galveston weekends like a school kid looked forward to vacations. At home he was in a state of perpetual motion, moving from one project to another. He spent a good deal of time on the computer with work-related projects. There were bills to pay, yard and house maintenance, and sandwiched in between all this was his running regimen.

He was a veteran of seven marathons. He took full advantage of his time in Galveston to bicycle, rollerblade, or run along the seawall. By evening, endorphins had secreted their magic, and he was as malleable as a marshmallow.

"Yes, we're going," I replied, "but Kanika was wondering if I could stay a little longer this time."

"Why, you all going to do something special?" he asked.

"Kind of," I said. "You know the baby I've been going to see in the hospital?"

Now it was his turn to take a drink of water. He set the glass down slowly. "Umm hum," he said.

"Okay, well . . . he's reached a stage now where he can leave the hospital, but they can't find anybody to take him." I rushed on. "He still needs a lot, and people are afraid they can't handle it. You know . . . they're afraid they might do something wrong, don't have the time, whatever. Kanika asked me if I'd be able to come stay with her for a while—help her take care of him—just until they can find a home. Of course, I told her I'd have to talk to you first. See how you felt about it."

I took a deep breath and waited. Even after all our years together, what I telegraphed and what he received often got lost in translation.

"How long are we talking about?" he asked

"Kanika said they told her they should be able to find somebody by October."

"That's over two months," he said, putting his fork down. Finally—*eye contact.*

"You remember the other day we talked about how quickly time passes and I joked how every meal seems like breakfast? It won't be that bad. You can come up every weekend; you've been saying how you'd like to go to the island more anyway." I could see his face starting to relax just considering that possibility. I continued quickly. "I just think as blessed as we've been with our own kids, this is the right thing to do. Give this baby a chance. Before you know it," I chirped, flashing my widest smile, "I'll be back home in time to cook a big Thanksgiving dinner."

"So when is all this going to happen?" he asked.

"Kanika is going to take care of him next week and . . ."

"And how's Kanika going to take care of anybody?" he asked.

"She's going 24/7 now."

"She's worked all that out," I replied. "Once I'm down there, she'll be able pick up right where she left off."

"It sounds like you guys have got it all worked out," he said. He stopped eating and the furrow between his brows deepened. The distance between us at the table seemed to lengthen.

"No, not really," I replied. "I told Kanika I wouldn't do it unless you agreed."

I watched him as he considered what I had said. His face softened. "You know," he began, "I remember when I was a little boy, I read a Bible story about a man who didn't help someone because he was afraid what it might cost him. Turned out, he ended up having a terrible life. I think you and Kanika are doing a good thing. Like you said, I can come down on weekends, and before we know it, you'll be home."

I called Nicole the next day and told her what I was planning. Nicole is my middle child, sandwiched in between the strong personalities and competitive spirits of her older brother and younger sister. Brought up in a family of focused and opinionated individuals, she has had to work at establishing a foothold in the path of our peculiar clan. She found her niche in outshining the rest of us as a people person, a social butterfly making friends wherever she flitted. Between her teaching and completing her master's, we stayed in touch mainly by phone. "How long will you be gone?" she asked.

"Until October." I hastily added, "You can come up with your dad on the weekends anytime you want to."

After a moment's silence, she said, "Are you sure you want to stay gone that long?"

"That's how long they say it's going to take for them to find someone."

"What about Dad?"

"We've talked about it. He's not crazy about me being gone, but he agrees it's the right thing to do."

Looking back, I'm struck by how easy it was to actually leave. I did not have to quit a job or a committee, leave a church or a friend. Our suburban neighborhood was typical of suburbia. People punched their garage door openers when their tires touched the driveway and disappeared. Except for my immediate family, I would not be missed. Throughout my life, I had left people, places, and things. As a child I learned to disappear in the midst of violence. Early in my husband's career, frequent job transfers necessitated that I be prepared both mentally and physically to move on. Although we had remained in Austin, I continued to maintain a transient mindset.

The lengths my family went to in order to support my decision to care for Baby B were both humbling and amazing. I have been married to the same man for more than three decades. "I know you like I know the back of my hand," I often told him. Yet I still underestimated his astounding generosity and unwavering commitment to our family. When you have been a mother since age twenty, and your children are grown with marriages and children of their own, you think there's nothing earth shattering left you can teach them or that they can teach you. You would be wrong.

I could never have imagined or predicted that Kanika's actions would catch me up and cast me into the middle of a miracle medical drama like a massive wave gathering along the

Galveston seawall. In the aftermath, the transformed seascape would change my concept of what I thought a family to be. It would change my concept of who I thought I was and who I really am. It would change the dynamics of our family circle forever.

CHAPTER 12

The Blessing

"We must have the stubbornness to accept our gladness in the ruthless furnace of this world."

—Jack Gilbert

"YOU GUYS MADE good time. No traffic tie-ups?" Kanika held the door open to the shotgun house, giving each of us a hug as we walked through it. She still wore her green surgical scrubs.

It was 10 p.m. on Friday, the summer moon so bright that it flooded the street like a searchlight. Lawrence had installed a porch light that automatically activated with any movement. Most of the time, it was just the ocean breeze blowing the tropical flora to and fro that caused the light to trigger. The city neglected installing sidewalks in our area, so the beam often caught people coming from the beach trampling across the yard so close to the house that we were startled by strangers appearing out of nowhere.

"Nope, we lucked out this time," I said. We had made the drive from Austin to Galveston Island in four hours. The I-10 traffic mishaps and construction detours routinely added another hour or two to the commute. We unpacked the car, having brought only a couple of overnight bags, our laptops, books, and papers. Then we collapsed on the couch, the captured audience of a commercial coming from the television. A woman was cheerfully sharing the serious side effects of a drug created to cure something. After hours of defensively dodging aggressive drivers and those paying more attention to their cell phones than the road, the mindlessly medicating effect of TV was welcome. Sometimes, it took a leap of faith just to back out of the driveway.

"So what's the plan for tomorrow, Kanika?" Lawrence asked. He was always thinking ahead. Like a chess player, as soon as he arrived at a place, he began planning the next move.

"Well," she said, "I finished all the arrangements today: signed papers, checked on his medications, made outpatient appointments with OT and PT. The car seat is in the car. I bought the kind that can transfer right from the car to the stroller. Mom and I will pick him up at nine in the morning. You don't have to go with us, Dad. Just stay here and relax. It shouldn't take that long."

I listened as Kanika ticked off details, envying her efficiency and her innate ability to act quickly with conviction. I guessed that this was what separated doctors, and more specifically surgeons, from the rest of us. Lawrence would have made an excellent doctor; he had those same qualities. I rarely felt as confident in my decision-making, but once I decided, I seldom changed my mind.

"Is everyone okay with you taking next week off?" I asked.

"I don't know about everyone, but it's okay with Dr. H, and he's the one that counts."

I knew from our past conversations that when residents took time off, it increased the caseloads of those remaining. Her answer reassured me that she had taken the necessary steps to protect her position on the team. I let the television numb my mind a while longer, before heading off to the spare bedroom.

* * *

At nine the next morning, Kanika and I walked through the revolving doors of Shriners Hospital. On Saturdays, no clinics or therapies were held. The elevator dinged open as soon as we pressed the button, carrying us swiftly up without stopping. The doors slid open to a silent, still corridor. On weekends, the frenzied hospital activity receded for a time, like outgoing tides. The lighting was muted, giving the hallways the same shadowy cast as a day ending. On the following Monday, all the rolling elements would rush back like incoming tides. The hallways would flood with people and the fluorescent light would strike the halls with the same stark brightness that assaulted the morning seashore. But Baby B would not be there.

We entered the gray aseptic room; I was still struck by its bareness. It was unsettling to walk in and find Baby B, motionless, looking complacently out into the emptiness like an elderly convalescent. He should have been moving, arms thrown wide, tottering toward the loving embrace of mirror arms. He should have been climbing toward his first birthday full of rambling curiosity.

I watched Kanika and the nurse disconnect all the conduits linked to his body, and listened to their small talk travel back and forth across the bed.

"Isn't it something how these things manage to coil around each other?"

"I'll hold this part while you pull that away."

They eventually extricated two central lines and a feeding tube.

"Being able to take that feeding tube out," Kanika told me later, "that was when I knew he was going to live."

Watching Kanika and the nurse as they untethered Baby B reminded me of my first visit when they placed him in my arms. Now as then, he offered no resistance. He seemed aware, alert, and wary, but he did not cry, whimper, or surrender any sound. He simply refused to succumb.

Shortly before we departed, the director of the The Children's Center, Inc., Craig, along with an older African-American woman, entered the room. Craig had coordinated Baby B's placement into Kanika's care, and then from her to me. He had a mop of white hair, soft gray eyes and an open, friendly manner. It seemed like every mature male on the island had a cap of snowy white hair, conspiring to turn gray rather than succumb to baldness. As I shook his hand, I recalled our conversation from weeks earlier. After I had completed the necessary paperwork, he sat back in his chair and said, "Well, that's it." He paused for a moment. "You know it's easy to get attached to these kiddos. You might not be ready to let him go by October."

"Oh, no, no, no," I replied quickly. "I've got three grown kids and three grandkids. A perfect balance. My maternal yearnings were satisfied a long time ago. I'm doing this because Kanika asked me to, and because this baby doesn't have anyone else. You need to have someone ready and waiting to take over by October. I have a husband and a life to get back to."

"Okay, okay," he had said, holding up both hands. "We'll keep looking."

"October," I repeated. "I promised my family I would be home in plenty of time for Thanksgiving."

He nodded his head in agreement.

Craig looked around the hospital room, rubbing his hands together. "Today's the big day. I'd like to introduce you to Mrs. Tate. She's the president of our board of directors."

Mrs. Tate, immaculately tailored and coiffed, looked as if

she had just exited the board room. A kind of regal aura surrounded her; Craig seemed genuinely pleased to be in her presence. "What a blessing," she said. "What a wonderful thing you all are doing for this baby. I just had to come and meet you myself."

After they left, Kanika and I finished gathering up bags of creams, ointments, medicines, salves, syringes, gauze, tapes, and bandages, and took leave with Baby B, our blessing.

PART II

A.B. (After Baby B)

CHAPTER 13

Esperanza

"Those eyes too pure and too honest in aught to disguise the sweet soul shining within."

—*Owen Meredith*

WHEN KANIKA AND I pulled up in front of the house, Lawrence was sitting on the porch with his computer. Kanika unbuckled the cradle seat and carried Baby B out of the scorching sun and up three wooden steps, and set him down in the cool shade of shelter. Baby B's hands, legs, and feet were still secured in splints and multiple wrappings, extending awkwardly out of the seat away from his body.

"Here he is, Dad," said Kanika. "This is Baby B."

"Hey, Baby," Lawrence said, smiling broadly and waving his hand in front of Baby B's face. Baby B looked past the hand into the face of this strange man. Baby B's eyes, already round and dark as the face of a black-eyed Susan, widened even more. A breeze pushed the bright blooms from a nearby esperanza bush onto the porch. *Esperanza* is Spanish for hope—exactly what we were feeling as we surrounded Baby B. It was the first time he had been out of a medically controlled environment since his evacuation from Mississippi. It was the first time he had been unchained from the cords connecting him to the mechanics of machines. For the first time in over a month, it was possible for him to see, feel, and hear the wonders of the natural world most of us take for granted: sunlight, not fluorescent light; air breeze, not air conditioning. Fluttering butterflies and buzzing bumblebees winged their way to pockets of golden pollen. Overhead, the sky stirred with seagulls screeching and circling crazily like rambunctious schoolchildren.

Lawrence touched the tips of Baby B's fingers, which poked from the bandages. "This looks a little different from the hospital, doesn't it, baby?"

I watched as they continued their examination of one another until Kanika returned from inside with Baby B's breakfast, a mushy concoction in a jumbo syringe.

"You want to feed him, Daddy?"

"Sure," Lawrence said. He placed the syringe gently in Baby B's mouth.

"Just give it to him in slow little pushes, Dad; he hasn't had any solid food in a long time."

And for the first time, Baby B took solid nourishment from a solid man who would love him solidly.

* * *

An undercurrent of excitement buzzed though the house. It reminded me of how I had felt each time I brought my own newborn home and realized that I was responsible for a brand new life. However, Baby B was not a newborn. He was now eleven months old. Unlike my babies, he did not like being held. Why would he? His body had changed forever. Perhaps he did not even recognize it as his own. We propped him on piles of blankets on the floor and surrounded him with pillows. We sat next to him and sang silly songs. We engaged in constant conversation around him so that he would become accustomed to our voices. He was unable to hold toys, so we held them up so that he could touch them. We carried him from room to room in his carriage seat several times a day, not only to familiarize him with the rooms in the house but also to experience the sensation of going from one place to another. His little body remained tense as if it were always anticipating some new assault . . . as if he were waiting for the other shoe to drop.

We realized that Baby B's transition from the volatility of the hospital to a household would be jolting. Therefore, we kept constant control of the inside activity and noise level. Outside, the summer tourist season was making its final August surge. Ambulances raced back and forth between the beach and the hospital, sirens blaring as they carried the last daredevils of the season.

Long ago at the church preschool my son attended, the children were taught to say a prayer whenever they heard an ambulance siren. I remembered hearing him whisper his petition in the backseat of the car one day as an ambulance sped by. It had brought tears to my eyes. But the sirens that wailed on the day we brought Baby B home broke open an uncharitable spasm of resentment in me. So what. That's what happens in life when you're having fun, I thought. Fall off your bike, slip off the pier, get struck by a surfboard, gash your foot running happily along the beach barefoot. So what. *Your* loved one didn't push you, or hit you, or cut you or beat you or burn you. *Your* friends and family will sit in the waiting room and comfort you. Hours later when the last stitch is sewn, the last doctor leaves, and the last paper is signed, you will leave with people who love and support you. Later, they will remind you of the great time you were having on Galveston Island when something rose up out of the murky deep and almost pulled you down, but family held on to you until you were safe.

* * *

"Hold it like this, place it toward the back, squeeze his jaws a little and shoot it in a bit at a time." Kanika was showing me how to administer Baby B's antibiotic. In addition to the hodge-podge of pureed nourishment we squirted into his mouth, he had to take a myriad of foul-tasting meds. He soon made the connection between content and size. Big syringe: yummy. Little syringe: yuk. As soon as he saw a little syringe raised and pointing, he pressed his lips tight, determined. Unable to fend us off with arms and hands bound in bandages, he became a champion at clamping those jaws shut, and spewing out the yuk with surprising force. After all he had been through, I hated having to force anything upon him. I was encouraged, however, to see that he had the cognitive ability to discern slight object differences, and that he still had the strength and willpower to resist.

We had crammed so much into the few hours since we had placed Baby B on the doorstep that morning. By the time the sun made its slow descent along the horizon into the sea, the sun worshippers had departed, and traffic had dispersed. The wails of ambulances grew farther and farther apart. We took Baby B back out to the porch, where the soft breezes of the morning had returned. The day's nectar-seeking insects had been replaced by evening's consortium of fireflies and crickets. Baby B fell asleep on nature's stage, surrounded by a symphonic production of original arrangements, full of lyrical sounds, far from the silent, stark hospital room.

* * *

We said our good-byes Sunday evening, and Lawrence and I drove back to Austin. We planned to return to Galveston the following Saturday so that I could assume care of Baby B and Kanika could resume her residency.

The drive hours were long, and the scenery stretching between Galveston Island and Austin began with weedy marshes and wasteland and turned to whatever you could glimpse of the small towns and cities from the complex connecting interstate highways. Preparing for the numbing drive ahead, I always paid particular attention when crossing the Galveston Bridge that connected the island to the mainland. As soon as I heard the "harrumph" in the road that signaled our ascent to the bridge, I sat a little straighter. A looming blue drawbridge came into view; its intricate design offered a sharp contrast to the humble island huts and beach houses lining the shore. Huge cargo ships and small fishing boats dotted the waters. Fishermen waded along the banks, throwing out their nets to ensnare live bait. Seagulls soared and sailed around the bridge, above the speeding cars, their *caw-caws* piercing the sky as they dipped and dived into the bay, beating the fishermen to prey.

I left the bridge behind, mentally preparing myself for the endless miles ahead. Lawrence sat in the passenger seat sticking plugs and adapters into sockets to power up his laptop. We shared driving duties. I usually drove the first two hours while he stared into his computer. He drove the next two hours while I read or slept, and in between we talked about the routine things that a long car trip tends to elicit: future vacations, past vacations, kids and grandkids, house repairs. The years were suddenly speeding past season after season, rushing us into a future that I could no longer view with the same elation and expectations of my youth. Time turned out to be a master thief.

After all his cords were inserted, Lawrence leaned back, fingers poised above the keyboard. "Are you okay?"

"Yes," I replied, somewhat defensively. "Why wouldn't I be?"
"Nothing, it just seemed liked you were drifting toward the other lane."

"No, I wasn't. Don't be a backseat driver. If you're going to supervise, you might as well drive." But he was right. I was drifting. I had started daydreaming as soon as Galveston Bridge appeared in the rearview mirror. The bridge had that effect on me—that magical moment suspended in air, when the sun sprayed its Fourth of July sparklers over the waterways below. Lawrence, aware that I was a daydreaming driver, knew that if he did not keep tabs on me that I might sail right past our exit. It had happened before, many times.

"I was just thinking about what to pack next week," I said.

"Not too much," he replied. "You don't want to have to drag a bunch of stuff back."

Whenever I made a statement about something I was planning or thinking, Lawrence's lexicon received it as a question and had a ready answer.

"It looks doable," I muttered.

"Yeah, I never pack a lot, just my running shoes and . . ."

"I mean taking care of Baby B," I replied quickly before he could give me his packing list. "I only heard Kanika get up with him once last night. This morning when I was helping her with him, he hardly cried at all. Of course, she gave him pain medication, so maybe he didn't feel much. And we didn't have to do anything with the bandages and splints he's wearing. She said they would do that when she took him to the tub room tomorrow."

"What's the tub room?" he asked.

"I guess it's where they change the bandages," I said. "Something like a doctor's examining room, maybe, with more supplies and stuff for burns." *Why hadn't the word* tub *alerted me? Why hadn't I made a connection between tub and water?*

During my years at the Veterans Hospital, even at the height of the Vietnam War, I never saw a veteran with burns. Then as now with the Gulf War, there were special burn hospitals for veterans. My encounter with the little girl in the pink cap on the elevator at Shriners was as close as I had ever come to anyone with burn scars. Though Baby B's face showed the strain of his hurting and isolation, it was still a baby's face, soft and beautiful. I had never seen the body hidden underneath bandages that I had cradled so carefully in my arms.

* * *

When we returned home, I stopped the newspaper and cancelled our reservations to the Big Bend National Park Lodge. The twin kayaks we had purchased for our river float hung unused, suspended from ropes in the garage. Each time I forgot to duck and collided with a kayak, I was reminded of how quickly my priorities had changed.

I gave the house a thorough cleaning and rearranged closets and drawers. I purged the refrigerator and scrubbed down the kitchen, wiping away the present, even as I walked into the future. I saw myself returning to find everything just as I had left it. No dust would settle while I was gone and the carpet would still reveal vacuum tracks. In a few months, I would walk directly back into the life I had left.

Knowing my husband, he would live out of two rooms, his office and the bedroom. He didn't know which knobs controlled the range. It was a good thing he liked cereal and peanut butter and jelly sandwiches. Growing up the oldest of ten children in rural Oklahoma, he had learned to make do.

Lawrence spent the majority of his evenings in his computer cave. We conducted many conversations at the doorway where I stood, one foot in and one foot out, ready to make my getaway. Lining the walls were thick technical manuals butted up against one another like sumo wrestlers. As we talked, he sat in his swivel chair, the upper part of his body turned toward me, the lower part twisted toward the computer, his eyes darting back and forth between me and the computer like a crack addict on the lookout for cops.

Now, as I crept past the room on my cleaning route, I pictured my husband rising from that chair in slow motion as I returned fresh from my mission in Galveston. He would be bleary-eyed and sluggish from the strain of computer screens and missing me as he stumbled toward me with open arms.

CHAPTER 14

Sea Glass

"Because there's nothing more beautiful than the way the ocean refuses to stop kissing the shoreline, no matter how many times it's sent away."

—*Sarah Kay*

LAWRENCE AND I returned to Galveston the following Saturday and stepped into a tranquil domestic setting. Kanika sat on the couch, cradling sleeping Baby B. All was quiet except for the low drone of the television.

"Hey, Mom," she said. "What's that?"

I held a large wicker basket filled with paints, brushes, and seashells. Earlier in the year, I had begun painting seascapes and creating beach crafts.

"My artwork," I replied. "I figured I could work on some things in my spare time."

"Good luck with that," she said.

"I'm used to juggling things. I'll have free time when he's sleeping like now," I replied curtly. Behind me, Lawrence entered, lugging travel bags, computers, and books.

"I'm just the pack horse," he quipped.

I caught a glimpse of my daughter's amused expression as I turned and flounced away.

"Do you want me to help you put him in his bed?" I had found a place for the basket in the little alcove that served as a laundry room and came back to find Kanika still holding Baby B. "You shouldn't keep holding him while he's sleeping," I admonished her. "He'll get used to it."

His little bed, situated at the foot of hers, was a portable collapsible child's bed easily moveable from one place to another. She placed him inside, and together we carefully positioned his arms and legs so that nothing poked or pressed against his tender body.

We exited the bedroom to find Lawrence sitting on the couch, holding a can of soda and flipping through a medical journal.

"Hey, Dad, see anything interesting in there?"

"The charts and graphs. If you ever need to do anything similar, I got a great program on my computer."

"Okay," she said smiling, "I'll remember that."

"How did you like staying home with a baby?" I asked. By the time I was her age, I had already been married and a mother for several years.

"It wasn't bad once I got into a routine."

"Did you miss being at the hospital?"

She shrugged. "The week passed pretty fast; hopefully I didn't miss much."

As usual, the house was spotless. The summer sunshine streamed through the slanted blinds, and all the familiar sounds and smells of the beach town seeped in. Were it not for the assortment of medications lining the kitchen counter, the presence of medical paraphernalia, a sick child sleeping in my daughter's bedroom, and the fact that I would be separated from my husband and living with my daughter for months, I could have almost talked myself into believing that I was there for an extended vacation.

* * *

Later, Lawrence and I watched Kanika gently wake Baby B from his nap. "Have to make sure he doesn't sleep too long or he's up at night," she said. I watched what she did closely, hoping to absorb her level of skill and confidence in handling his hurt body. After all, she knew far more than I did about him. I was the expert when it came to my children. But when it came to Baby B, I was a novice. She had stood by his bedside at Shriners. Now he slept at her bedside.

He woke slowly, his eyes blinking, becoming still as he surveyed the three faces staring into his. Kanika laid him on the bed and began changing his diaper. He let out a low, incessant whimper. I remembered his cries in the hospital coming in short, quick expulsions of protest as if he didn't have the strength for sustained outbursts. She pulled the cloth diaper away. Cloth was used instead of disposable to avoid any irritants to his skin and discarded immediately to lessen the chances of contamination. She examined his bottom closely for several minutes.

"Something wrong?" asked Lawrence.

"Yeah," replied Kanika. "I need to cauterize some spots."

"What does that mean?" I asked.

"Scar tissue I need to take off before it hardens."

"Anything you want me to do?" Lawrence asked.

"I need you to hold him still," she said. "Mom, can you get the pain medicine?"

She pulled a small slender package from a sack of supplies. Inside it was a silver nitrate stick. The stick acted as a cauterization agent to destroy dead tissue.

I left the room.

After a while the screams subsided. Lawrence brought Baby

B out to me, and I held him until he drifted back to sleep. It was my first introduction to the parade of procedures that would parallel the path Baby B and I traveled together.

* * *

On Sunday morning, Lawrence and I walked to the seawall and descended the steps to the beach. The sun shone so brilliantly that it was if the sky, sand, and sea were in the sway of a kaleidoscope. Pebbles shimmered in the shallow water like fool's gold. Stranded jellyfish glistened on their deathbed of imported sand. Several times a year huge truckloads of sand were hauled in overnight to replenish beach that the sea sought to reclaim. Bulldozer headlight beams spread across the shore like rays of invading spaceships. Giant scoop shovels transferred the sand from one place to another until the fantasy of a natural beach was restored.

Lawrence and I watched vendors setting up chairs and umbrellas. Hotel guests from across the street dodged traffic, leaving their pristine hotel swimming pools to get sand in their swimsuits and submerge themselves in the murky Gulf water. We turned and headed in the opposite direction, sloshing along the water's edge with our plastic bags. I searched for sea glass while Lawrence looked for seashells.

"Look," I said, spotting a glass chip. I stooped down and picked up the red piece—a rare color find—and held it up. "See how smooth the edges are? No jagged or sharp points. All that rough tossing back and forth has made it more beautiful. Would you believe there are machines that make fake sea glass?"

"Why don't you buy one?" Lawrence asked, smiling. "It could save us a lot of time. Then we could just go rent one of those beach chairs and flop down for the morning."

"I'm sure you'd love that," I said. "Somebody who can't sit still for five minutes. Instead of looking for shells, why don't you just walk down to the gift shop and buy a bag of plastic shells for a dollar?"

"Why should I give them my hard-earned dollar when I can get the real thing here for free?" he replied. We laughed and continued canvassing the beach. In the distance, sandpipers skittered in and out of the low tide, playing dodge with the waves.

"What are you going to do when you get back to Austin this evening?" I asked.

"Feed the dog. Cut the grass, if it's not too late. Pay bills. Computer work."

"Well, try to get to bed before the sun comes up," I replied sarcastically. My husband required remarkably little sleep, while I did not feel fully sane unless I got eight hours. I wondered if we were an oddity among couples, who, after decades of marriage, still had not managed to synchronize sleeping patterns.

That afternoon, we walked from the house to his car. "I'll see you Friday," he said. We kissed good-bye. I stood on the porch and watched my husband drive away.

CHAPTER 15

No Tears

"Have a heart that never hardens and a temper that never tires, and a touch that never hurts."
—*Charles Dickens*

M Y BED AT the Galveston cottage was a foldout couch in the back bedroom. Kanika and Baby B occupied the front bedroom. Baby B woke only once that night. Through the tiny connecting bathroom, it took me less than twenty steps to reach their room to help her with his bottle and diaper. Luckily he went right back to sleep since we all had to be at the hospital at eight the next morning.

I set my alarm for six. I was a slow starter and wanted to make sure I was out of the bathroom before Kanika zipped through. Unlike my feet, Kanika's seemed to have electrical charges, energized as soon they struck the floor. I had not shared a bathroom in years—not even with my husband. As soon as she left for college, I moved all my things from the master bathroom to the hall bathroom. It was one of our keys to a happy marriage.

Kanika and I dressed quickly so that we could devote most of our time to Baby B. "Wear something cool," she suggested. "It's hot in the tub room."

I dressed Baby B while she assembled his various medications and prepared his bottle. The medicines needed to be given early enough so they would have optimum effect by the time we reached the tub room.

Outside, the August sun, heat, and humidity combined to cast a heavy haze. I pulled into the hospital's circular driveway, and Kanika went inside to obtain a token from the desk attendant for patient parking. I jumped out, opened the back of my SUV, and extracted the outsized stroller, wrestling it to the ground. I fumbled around, trying to unfold the thing. It had been twenty-plus years since I had done anything but pass one on the street. This multi-use monster had numerous gadgets, pulleys, and knobs. *What fresh new hell is this?*

Kanika, back with the token, saw me struggling, walked over, and extended the contraption with one swift jerk. I summoned what little pride I could corral and pushed Baby B through the revolving doors of the hospital (another major maneuver) while Kanika parked the car.

We took the elevator up and waited outside the double doors leading to the tub room. The sleeveless floral summer dresses we wore contrasted with the dull gray walls of the long, narrow corridor. We were daisies sprouting from cement. There was an ominous, gloomy aura permeating the area. Unlike the other bustling hallways in the hospital, there was no activity. Standing in the hallway, I must have exhibited some unease because Kanika asked if I was okay.

"Yes," I said. "I was just wondering why it's so quiet here."

Before she could reply, a nurse dressed in dark scrubs pushed open the heavy door.

"We're ready now," said the nurse, a tall woman with inky black hair pulled back at the nape of the neck. Her severe demeanor seemed to hold every piece in place. She held the door open with her back and watched us file past with Baby B.

The windowless room reeked of bleach and was flooded with stark, white light. Chromatic light bounced off the stainless steel fixtures and instruments. Glass-fronted cabinets filled with medical supplies abutted the upper walls. More cabinets lined the walls at floor level. Two mammoth stainless steel vats, hollowed-out gray elephants, occupied opposite sides of the room. Hoses coiled around the upper rims. The room was oppressively warm and humid. The temperature had to be maintained above ninety degrees to maintain body temperature of patients who no longer had the cover of skin.

Kanika placed Baby B on the examining table. I stood beside him while she circulated the room, collecting supplies. Another nurse entered the room, and the woman who had ushered us in exited.

"Hey, Kanika. You guys ready?" the new nurse asked. He perused the room, opening and closing cabinets and drawers, draping towels over tables.

"Just about," she replied, handing me a gown and gloves. "It's a little early for you, isn't it?"

"Yeah," he replied. "Short-handed again."

"This is my mom."

"Hi, Mom," he said, without looking my way.

Not your mom, hers. I registered an instant dislike for him. I found myself in a situation for which I was ill-prepared, and the casualness of it all agitated me.

Kanika and I stood on each side of the table, Baby B between us. As I slipped on my gown and gloves, she picked up a pair of scissors and started snipping the bandages at the edges of his toes.

"Start here like this," she said. *Surely, she doesn't expect me to do that.*

I watched her lift Baby B's leg with one hand and with the other hand take the bandage over and under, smoothly and expertly. I braced myself for the sight of burnt flesh, but instead a layer of white fabric appeared.

"What's that?" I asked.

"Gauze. It's a barrier to keep the Ace bandage from irritating his wounds," she said. "It'll have to be soaked off in the tub." Baby B was quiet and compliant, his meds obviously working for now. I slowly unraveled the Ace bandage on the other leg, like peeling a grapefruit.

"You can do it a little faster, Mom. You're not going to hurt him."

Not convinced, I fought hard to keep my hands from trembling. I felt clumsy and inept, a feeling that would become so familiar that I would rejoice in its absence. We cut away the last strip and added it to the piles littering the table like miniature anthill mounds. Free of the encasing, Baby B's small, naked body came into focus. I steeled myself against the sight. Third-degree burns do terrifying damage, destroying three layers of protection for the body—skin, tissue, and muscle. My resolve not to cave into emotion kept me numb, much like the meds that kept Baby B from crying out.

"Okay, we're ready," said Kanika, gently lifting him into her arms.

She crossed the room to the tub, and I backed away, heading in the opposite direction until I felt my back hit the wall.

I watched as the nurse reached across and helped Kanika lower Baby B into the tub, positioning him with a body support so that their hands were free to accomplish the task quickly.

"Get ready, guy. This is going to hurt you more than us," quipped the nurse.

Two overhead hoses uncoiled downward, creeping tentacles, gushing out warm water. Kanika and the nurse directed the water onto Baby B, alternately soaking and scrubbing him with antibacterial soap and pads, a debridement procedure. It was done in order to minimize infection and scarring. There is pain that drugs cannot prevent. The crying commenced.

I watched and listened from my wallflower position while they sprayed and scrubbed. Sprayed and scrubbed. "So when are you coming back to work?" the nurse asked, his words seeping through the cacophony of sounds.

"I'm back," Kanika answered.

"Hey, Mom," the nurse said, looking at me. "You might as well come over and join the fun. You're going to have to do this eventually."

"I'll pass," I said, hating him. *And stop calling me Mom.*

"Come on, Mom," said my daughter. "Come help me."

I took my place beside my daughter, not wanting to embarrass her. These were people she had to work with every day. She put the antibacterial soap on a pad and handed it to me. "Apply enough pressure to rub away as much dead skin as you can."

I began. I listened to Baby B's screams as if from a distance. I avoided looking into his face. I concentrated on the section I scrubbed as if peering through the eye of a camera. The heat in the room and the gurgling of the water streaming from the hose mingled with the sound of Kanika's voice, guided me through the terrible terrain, and shrouded time. When people say, "I don't know how you did it," I remember that moment and others like it. I believe that the only reason I persevered was because I was held firmly in place by the grip of grace. The kind of grace that offered me an internal escape when a physical one was not possible.

"What do you think, Kanika?" asked the nurse. "Ready to move on?" As he spoke, he gathered the soggy gauze and dead skin swirling in the waterbed, tossing them in a nearby bin.

"Sure," she said, lifting Baby B and carrying him across

the room to an area where the next phase of treatment would proceed. We regrouped to rewrap Baby B: arms, hands, fingers, torso, legs, feet, toes. Jars, tubes, topical ointments, and antibiotics lined the counter. One jar contained a yellow, thick, slick substance of Polymyco, a topical antimicrobial cream that destroys or inhibits the growth of microorganisms that could cause disease. We cut twenty tiny strips of gauze, slathered them with cream, and wrapped a strip around each tiny finger and toe. We cut and prepared more gauze for his legs, arms, and hands.

"We always start the bandage at the feet and work our way up," Kanika said. "Take it up and down and around in a figure eight to keep the circulation going upward and to prevent pressure points.

I tried to mirror her movements.

Baby B had reached his pressure point and was squirming and screaming at full scale.

"The medicine must be wearing off," I said.

"It's supposed to last at least three hours," said Kanika.

"Oh, he's not hurting; he's just pissed off because we're messing with him," said the nurse.

"How do you know that?" I asked.

"Look at his face. No tears. If he were really hurting, there would be tears."

I heard these words repeated numerous times at different stages of his treatment, and it never failed to infuriate me. Is someone not shedding tears in the midst of grief not grieving? It is hurt that cannot be expressed outwardly that is the most excruciating. There is no outlet, and so the tears are trapped where they swell up and flood the inside.

Finally two hours later, with Baby B sloughed, slathered in salves, and swaddled in layers of bandages, we departed from the tub room. Of all the dark tunnels an individual or family will traverse for burn treatment, the tub room is universally described as the most heart-wrenching and exhausting. During operations and skin grafts, patients are anesthetized, and their families are spared having to witness or participate. Those barriers disappear when they cross the threshold to the tub room. A family member or caretaker has to participate in order to be able to perform the treatment at home once the patient was released. Although patients receive medication, they can never be sedated enough to eliminate the searing sensation of abrasives assaulting exposed flesh.

Parents who normally comfort their child post-surgery and are surrounded and supported by hospital staff are now expected to stand beside seasoned professionals and participate in a torturous process. Possibly, nothing else in their lives will ever compare. Some parents, overcome by their child's suffering and their own contribution to that suffering, run from the room. But eventually it is a rite of passage every parent or caretaker of a seriously burned child must endure.

As we drove home, Baby B, depleted from the ordeal, slept in his car seat. Although it was barely 10 a.m., the tropical sun blazed like a fireball. The day was just beginning.

"Boy, he was a piece of work," I said.

"Who?" Kanika asked, pulling to a stop in front of the bungalow.

"That nurse. What a jerk with his no tears, no pain theory."

"I don't think he meant any harm; that's just his way," she said.

"Do you really think he believes that?"

"What?"

"That no tears no pain crap."

"I don't know, Mom, but that's probably how he copes with that job. Nobody else wants to do it. That's why they're always shorthanded."

"And I don't like him calling me *Mom*. I'm not old enough to be his damn *mom*.

"Okay," she said, shrugging her shoulders. "Tell him that."

Kanika helped get Baby B and me settled before she hurried back to the hospital. I closed the door behind her, drew the blinds against the heat of the day, and collapsed into bed next to the baby's crib. That day Kanika resumed her full duties as a resident. Although she called to check on us, it would be ten hours before she walked through the door again.

* * *

The next morning as she was leaving, Kanika said, "It's real important that you get there on time. One person late makes all the other appointments run late."

Rising in the gray dawn to begin the day's trek alone filled me with dread. Yesterday, Kanika had been my trail guide through the perilous hallways of the hospital hierarchy and the horde of minutia. Today I would have to hack through it by myself, carrying a fragile bundle.

I pulled to a stop in the hospital's circular driveway, got out, and rushed through the revolving doors to obtain a token for the parking lot. "Good morning," I said to the desk attendant, a paunchy, grizzled man sitting behind the reception desk.

"You can't park there," he said, pointing toward the window.

"I know," I said. "I just need a token."

"A token for what?"

"The patient parking lot," I said, smiling and holding out my hand.

"There's pay parking down the street. We don't just hand out tokens to anybody."

"I have a child that's due for an appointment in the tub room in a few moments," I said. He stood up, placed his two palms on the countertop, and peered over it.

"Where is he?"

"He's in the car," I said. He sat back down, pulled open a drawer, extracted the token, and deposited it into my outstretched hand—a prince placing a coin in the hands of a pauper. He exaggerated his every move in a show of superiority. I turned and walked out of the lobby on the verge of tears. I parked, wrestled the mammoth stroller from the SUV, unlatched the carrier, attached it to the stroller, and speed-walked the block back to Shriners, through the revolving doors, up the elevator, and down the hall to the tub room. We were late.

I knocked on the gray double door and waited. "Sorry we're late," I said to the same nurse guarding the door the day before. Not bothering to reply, she pivoted and walked to the exam table and watched as I dislodged Baby B from his stroller and placed him on the table. "We wouldn't have been late, but the guy at the desk downstairs took his own sweet time about giving me a token for the parking lot." She and I began unwrapping Baby B's bandages. My voice was strained and my hands trembled. Perhaps she noticed because her manner softened.

"What did he look like?" she asked.

"Short guy, dark hair, glasses."

"Bald, swarthy-looking?" she asked.

"Yes," I said.

"Umm. I think I know who it is," she said. "There've been other complaints. They just keep moving him around."

"Well," I said, "I guess he has a job he can excel at, intimidating families of burn kids." With that, all talking ceased and we concentrated on the business at hand. She was unflinchingly efficient and quick. When I pointed out with timidity a piece of skin that had escaped abrasion, her pincher fingers darted out like a reptile's tongue and flicked it away. "Better to be quick and get it over with," she said. We were wrapping gauze around the last little toe, careful to avoid the pins that had been inserted to secure the joints against contractions caused by burn. Baby B was in full-scale scream mode when she said, "He's not hurting; he's just mad we're messing with him." At least she didn't call me *Mom*.

That night I told Kanika about my hassle getting a parking token. "Call me on my cell phone when you get there if it happens again," she said.

I set my alarm to go off even earlier the next morning so that Baby B and I would be sure to make it to the tub room on time. The same attendant watched me as I approached the counter.

"You can't park there."

"I'm not parking; I need a token for the parking lot."

"Those are for patients."

"We went through this yesterday," I said. "He's in the car."

"What time is your appointment? What floor is it on?"

"Are you going to give me the third degree every morning I come in here?"

"That's my job."

"Yeah, well my job is to get him to the tub room on time," I said, holding out my hand. He stood up slowly, deposited the rustic token in the middle of my palm—alms to the pauper.

I called Kanika when I returned to the car. "He's at it again," I said.

"Okay," she said. "I'm coming."

By the time I parked, unfurled the stroller, and pushed Baby B into Shriners, Kanika, the desk attendant, and two men wearing dress jackets and ties were standing in the lobby deep in conversation. I didn't stop. My daughter didn't look like she needed my help. That evening she gave me a magnetic card that I could swipe at the parking lot entrance so that I never had to go with my hand out to that man again. But I felt for the other families walking in, carrying the pain of their hurt children who would be blocked by that troll.

CHAPTER 16

Ready or Not

"By morning I had vanished at least a dozen times into something better."

—*Mary Oliver*

I T HAD FAILED to register when the nurse suggested that I should participate in the tub treatments because soon it would be my responsibility. It never occurred to me at the time that I was in boot camp for a solo mission.

"Do you think you're ready to do the tub treatments now?" asked Kanika one evening.

"You mean by myself?"

"Yes, you can do it here. You wouldn't have to go to Shriners."

I would not have to go to Shriners. I would not have to rise at dawn pressured to get Baby B dressed and fed and medicated and out the door by 7 a.m. No racing to and from the parking lot, loading and unloading the monster stroller that threatened to overtake me each time I grappled it to the ground. No more lifting it over curbs that were not handicapped accessible even though the route from the parking lot led directly to the hospital. In one particularly dangerous area, this meant having to push the stroller into the street facing oncoming traffic until we regained access to the sidewalk, where we were assaulted by billows of caustic cigarette smoke coming from hospital employees on their break. Most importantly, I would be able to conduct Baby B's bath treatments and skin care in a calm environment with no negative attitudes or insensitive comments. "Yes," I answered. "I'm more than ready." That night, Kanika instructed me in the treatments I would need to perform without being under the guidance of seasoned professionals. We gathered the bath solutions, soaps, assorted antibacterial topical preparations, gauze, and bandages. I practiced the figure eight bandaging technique on Kanika's arm until I felt I could perform the rotation in my sleep. Together, we cut dressing into the strips that I would use to wrap Baby B's body and each of his fingers and toes.

*　*　*

Before departing for the hospital the next morning, Kanika came into my room. "I'm leaving, Mom. You and Baby B have the whole day to yourselves. Call me if you need anything. Love you."

"I will," I said. "Love you." I heard the creak of the floorboards as she walked to the front door and thought of the many footsteps from a century past that had crisscrossed the ancient planks of the old house. I turned to my side and thought about my husband. He routinely left the house at dawn in an attempt to beat the Austin I-35 traffic juggernaut. At home, I often awoke with a jolt to find him gone, the pillow imprinted with his weight. What did he awaken to in my absence?

I lay in bed a little longer and listened to the old house moan as its decrepit joints shifted. *If these walls could talk.* I breathed in the musty breath of the house that Lawrence tried to erase with scented candles and plug-ins. The island's rising sun seeped through the blinds, flooding the room with a golden glow. Foghorns from cruise ships docking in Galveston Harbor sounded in the distance. Lawrence and I had taken two cruises, one celebrating our twenty-fifth wedding anniversary and another celebrating Nicole's college graduation. Both times were full of great memories, but the sound of ships' horns no longer beckoned me. I had reached the conclusion long ago that being cloistered in a confined area and shuffled about on a schedule was something life provided plenty of for free.

I threw back the covers and went to peek at Baby B. By that time, we had moved his crib into a small alcove adjacent to my room.

He was still. I laid my hand on his chest to assure myself that he was still breathing. Craving coffee, I slouched to the kitchen, ready for my fix, only to discover the carafe empty because I had omitted the final step in the setup. Deflated, I flipped the switch, leaned against the counter, and watched the dark liquid dribble down while I listened to the calm, congenial voice of an NPR commentator report the latest terrorist threat, mass murder, and other miscellaneous mayhem.

When the coffee was ready, I sat at the little table and looked out the window onto the backyard. The same sandy soil that constantly shifted on the beach stayed stagnant in yards. Consequently, yards were grittier and dirtier, full of cockleburs and tough brown roots that spiraled into the ground like steel drills, seeking the center of the earth. The weedy, barren patch I had once surveyed from the garage apartment next door was now a tropical oasis. Once Kanika moved in, Lawrence and I hauled in fertile soil to marry with the dry, gritty sand and planted drought-resistant, heat-tolerant, tropical hibiscus, brilliant birds-of-paradise, and prickly cacti. I could see purple periwinkles poking through the pregnant soil.

*   *   *

I finished my coffee and reluctantly returned to my room to arrange things for Baby B's treatment. I straightened the covers on the pullout couch that was my bed and topped it with worn white sheets from the hospital. I placed everything that Kanika and I had gathered the night before within arm's reach of the bed, and I checked and double-checked supplies. Then I headed for the bathroom to bleach down the tub and organize bath solutions and towels. Back in the kitchen, I turned the radio dial to the soothing sound of classical music and took a deep breath.

For a moment, I stood over Baby B, watching him sleep. Then I slipped my hands underneath his little body and lifted him from his crib, cradling him in my arms. Holding him against me, I felt the angular jaunt of the plastic mold taped to his hand to prevent contractions press hard against my breast. His eyes slowly opened and fixed on my face with the same perplexity they always seemed to project when he was coming into consciousness.

I felt his body stiffen and shift as it strained to adjust to a series of sensations. "Good Morning, Baby B," I murmured, as I carried him to my room. "It's just you and me today."

I squirted pain medicine into his mouth and held him as he drank from his bottle. Soon he seemed relaxed enough for me to begin removing his bandages. Mellow music streamed from the radio. I relaxed with him into the moment. I recalled Kanika saying that surgeons often brought their favorite music to play in the operating room. Suddenly I understood why. Music can be both grounding and releasing.

I laid Baby B on the sheet, took up the scissors, and began to cut away the bandages, thankful once again that I was not at the hospital trapped in a space that sapped my strength and the penetrating light that illuminated my insecurities.

I snipped and unwrapped, snipped and unwrapped until the small wastebasket was filled with bandages. Throughout the process, Baby B protested mildly, but now with his body bare, no longer protected by the materials that acted as a barrier against the strange sensation of air surrounding him, he began to twist and twitch as if his body were under siege.

I covered him quickly with a sheet before he could get a chill and carried him into the warm bathroom. Normally, central air would have been cooling the house that hot August morning, but I had set the thermostat to simulate the warm environment of the tub room.

I centered a blue infant tub cushioned with towels inside the bathtub. I lowered Baby B onto the infant tub partially submerged in warm water and got down on my knees. "You're okay, you're okay," I whispered as I cupped water in my palms and let it flow through my fingers over him. He began to whimper, the whimpers escalating to wails. I asked myself the same question I had the first time I held him at the hospital. *What can I say or do to ease his pain?* Taking him out of the water was not an option. We would just have to start the whole process over again.

I continued trying to soothe him with words even as I scoured dead skin away. I sensed more than pain was causing him to suffer. He seemed filled with fear—*of me.* His terror was as palpable as a punch, a jab to my heart. He recoiled from my touch. His arms and legs flailed the water. What I saw as I looked into his eyes was not my own reflection, but *her image.* It broke my heart to think he was reliving that horror, and I was serving as stand-in for her unspeakable act. With that realization, I began to sob. Tears fell in torrents down my face into the murky water, mixing with his.

At Shriners' tub room, surrounded by others, I had neither the responsibility nor authority to respond to Baby B's pain. However, trapped alone in the tiny bathroom, all of those barriers were blown apart as his screams ricocheted off the walls. I could dodge none of it. I tried to will myself into that surreal state where I could float above the moment in order to complete the task at hand, but escape was not possible. We were both going under.

His eyes locked onto mine with a look of sheer terror.

I grabbed the phone. "I can't do this," I cried. "I can't. I thought I could, but I can't!" I had lifted Baby B from the water and was sitting on the bathroom floor with him, wrapped in a towel, still thrashing on my lap.

"Mom? What's the matter?"

How must we have sounded, baby and I both shrieking in a hysterical chorus.

"I'm trying to bathe him, and it's hurting him so much. He just keeps screaming. I know he thinks I'm *her* . . . that it's happening all over again!"

"Okay, it's okay," she said. "Don't worry. You don't have to do it anymore. I'll call the tub room and see if they can get him in today, and then I'll come straight home as soon as I can get away. Okay?"

"Okay," I replied feebly. I hung up the phone dismayed that the morning had turned disastrous so quickly despite all my careful preparations. Somehow, I got through the next few hours. I felt a mixture of relief and disappointment in myself when Kanika walked through the door, gathered Baby B and me up in her efficient but loving arms, and carted us back to the hospital.

* * *

One morning two weeks later, I returned with Baby B to find a different nurse preparing the tub room. She welcomed me with a wide, warm smile. "Hey, how are you guys doin'? Let's get this show on the road so you all can get on with the rest of your day." I liked her immediately. Dark coiffed hair framed her caramel brown face, and lively hazel eyes embraced Baby B and me. Sylvia wore a bright scrub top crisscrossed with cartoon characters and moved with jovial exuberance. I wondered how she managed to maintain her upbeat, positive attitude in the midst of ongoing misery. She did not espouse the "no tears, no pain" philosophy. "If they're still cryin', then they're still feelin.' Cryin' ain't always a bad thing." She had worked in the burn unit for twenty-five years, much of that time spent in the tub room. She was compassionate and considerate. Her self-effacing humor was so contagious that I caught myself laughing, grateful that I still could.

"So how did your daughter talk you into this?" she asked, as we smoothed salves over Baby B's body. You need a vacation?" She chuckled.

I gave her a brief history of how I had arrived at the present. For the first time since I entered the room, she didn't have a quick response. We worked in silence for a moment, all of our attention directed toward Baby B. Then she shared her story. "My only daughter has been dead three years now. This guy broke into the house one night. Murdered her. My three grandbabies were asleep. I'm raising them now."

"I'm sorry," I said, seeing the sadness flooding her face.

"Thank you. We're doing good, though," she said, a smile slipping back onto her face. "The youngest is five. They keep me and my husband busy and . . . happy."

Even though the tub room remained the last place on earth I would ever want to be, I gained a new level of respect and became less judgmental of the nurses who walked through those double doors every day. I made two more trips to the tub room before I felt sufficiently skilled and emotionally stable enough to accept the fact that in order to help Baby B, I would have to travel with him through the pain.

As time passed, I met more Shriners employees like Sylvia who had not become jaded by their surroundings and always had a smile and an encouraging word for children and parents, who God knows needed it. One could see in the eyes of the parents how haunted they were by what had happened to their children. And the children's eyes reflected the heartsickness and despondency they saw in their parents. They all seemed shell-shocked. In a flash, their entire lives were transformed. Most of the children's burns were caused by a sudden explosion or fire. One moment they possessed the smooth, vibrant bodies of youth. The next moment they were trapped in searing pain and the restricted bodies of old age.

In subsequent months I sometimes saw Sylvia scurrying down the hall on her way to another hurting child. She always exuded energy and openness that I never ceased to admire. Whenever she ran into me, her eyes widened. She smiled broadly, raised her arms in surprise, and belted out two questions: "You still here?" and "You still married?"

"Yes" and "still," I replied, laughing.

I appreciated her good-natured inquiries because she seemed to be the only person around who recognized me as an individual, separate from my caretaker role. Her second question pertaining to my marriage might have contained a subtle warning. Studies show that many marriages fall apart when challenged by a critically ill child. When burn is involved, the chance of a marriage surviving is at even greater risk. Burns in children occur either of two ways: intentional or accidental. If the burn is intentional, as a result of abuse, the authorities are summoned and a forced removal of the child or abuser takes place. If the burn is accidental or caused by carelessness on the part of one or both parents or a random event like a car crash or a house fire, parents may blame themselves or each other. Couple the emotional upheaval with the financial and physical realities involving years of surgeries, hospitalizations, and rehabilitation, and even those unions built on a strong foundation and commitment are in danger of collapsing under the constant pressure.

Had my marriage been similarly challenged, I might not have been able to laugh along with Sylvia, but her good-natured teasing was a welcome diversion. And unlike other parents at Shriners, I labored under the belief that the days I spent trudging back and forth to the hospital would end in months, not years. Ironically, I looked forward to talking with Lawrence about domestic routines at home more than I ever had before. I peppered him with questions about the most mundane of things: "How much junk mail today?" "Was the neighbor's dog still yelping at night?" "How was traffic?"

The calls from my husband and Nicole reminded me that my former life was still in Austin, waiting for me. The sound of their voices was like touching solid ground after stepping off a roller coaster. For a brief time, I could get my balance before being zapped up and tossed back into the abyss. Although Lawrence always asked about my day, I answered him in generalities, putting on a brave voice. I did not want to burden him with details of my lonely, desolate days.

I also tried keeping the conversation light with Nicole, but she and I had always been able to detect the nuances in each other's voices. As soon as she said, "Are you okay? You sound tired," the floodgates opened. I purged about the long, lonely days, about Baby B's night terrors that went on for hours, about the constant caretaking, and about the exhausting trips back and forth to the hospital. She listened as I cried and complained about my inability to comfort Baby B and my sadness and anger that my best never seemed good enough. These conversations marked a substantial turning point in how Nicole and I related to each other. She had always come to me for advice and guidance. And though her independence increased with the years, I freely offered opinions, admonishing, counseling, and delivering chicken soup. Now that I was the one in need, she became the person with whom I could vent. She listened with empathy and encouraged me without forecasting rosy resolutions.

Each day was an endurance run. I stumbled forward, placing one foot in front of the other. I was exhausted, but I refused to acknowledge it. If I did, I might simply collapse. My appetite ceased. Afternoons arrived before I realized I had consumed nothing but morning coffee. Dinner was a snack, foraged from the refrigerator. From the time I stumbled out of bed in the morning until I crumbled back into it at night, my singular focus was on maintaining the schedule of treatments, therapies, and medications fundamental to Baby B's recovery. At times, I did not even have the strength to change into my bedclothes.

The routines I had established over a lifetime disappeared. Exercise, which I had always needed to stay balanced, vanished. On the odd evenings Kanika was home, she tried to convince me to go for a walk on the beach or at least to go sit on the seawall. "You know you always feel better afterward," she said. But I retreated to the silence of my room.

Although I no longer had to take Baby B to Shriners for tub treatments, it became necessary to increase his baths to twice a day to further lessen the chance of infections as his skin healed. Alone each morning, the treatment took me three hours. It was still an intimidating task. I still believed that he was having flashbacks of the abuse, but it had to be done. I concentrated on staying calm and being as gentle as possible while performing procedures that were anything but. After the tub treatment, I spent the remainder of the day keeping him comfortable, medicated, and nourished. Making sure he got adequate nourishment was especially important because burn patients expend twice as many calories because their cells are constantly regenerating and repairing skin, tissue, and muscle. I felt increased anxiety as time passed about my overwhelming responsibilities. After watching a court TV segment about a daycare worker on trial for killing a child with an overdose of Tylenol, I became compulsive about checking and rechecking his medication doses. I worried about Kanika coming home from the hospital after putting in a twelve- to fifteen-hour day and having to help me with Baby B's second tub treatment. Working together, it took us over two hours. If Baby B was more agitated than usual and we had to go slower or stop for a while, it took much longer.

We were both under tremendous pressure. I, however, did not have to be at the hospital constantly. In addition to performing her duties as a resident, Kanika shared the responsibilities of caring for Baby B with me when she returned home. Although we both were teetering on the edge, we never turned on each other.

CHAPTER 17

Riding It Out

Greek legend says that Pandora, the first mortal woman, received from Zeus a box that she was forbidden to open. The box contained all human blessings and all human curses. Temptation overcame restraint, and Pandora opened it. In a moment, all the curses were released into the world, and all the blessings escaped and were lost— except one: Hope.

I BECAME FASTER AT the bath treatments, and though Baby B continued to roil against the process, he allowed me to cuddle and comfort him afterward. That helped ease the nagging guilt I felt about the physical and emotional pain he endured.

The schedule intensified in September when he began receiving daily physical therapy (PT) at Shriners. Although I had become adept at running the obstacle course from house to the hospital, PT was a new hurdle. I had to circle the entire fourth floor twice before finding it and catapulting the stroller forward before the hydraulic door clamped closed. *What was a hydraulic door doing at the entrance to the rehab room?*

Eventually I learned to throw my derriere against the door while propelling the stroller forward.

I signed in at the reception window and took a seat in one of the plastic chairs aligned along the wall. Baby B, ever vigilant, sat stoically in the stroller, surveying the surroundings with a mixture of curiosity and caution.

The physical therapist appeared and led us into a large rehabilitation room past a smaller glass-fronted, self-contained area to a low platform therapy table in the corner. Toys were piled on shelves and in large plastic bins. Therapists worked with children of varying ages, guiding them through exercises. The room hummed with activity. One therapist played table games with several adolescents, encouraging them to extend their arms and "reach through the pain."

"If you want to hug that girlfriend of yours again, you better start stretching that arm."

Another therapist stood in front of a small girl, holding her hands as the child took tiny wooden steps.

At the therapist's instruction, I removed Baby B from the stroller and placed him on my lap. "Scoot back," she directed, "and sit him on the inside of your legs so his back and sides are supported. I'm Claire," she said, as she surveyed Baby B, touching him lightly here and there. She was a petite, young woman, with chestnut hair and soft gray eyes. "You must be Kanika's mom," she said.

"Yes. Cynthia."

"We'll be able to work with him a lot better here than in that hospital bed," said Claire.

"Oh, you saw him as an inpatient?" I asked.

"Oh yeah. We start working with them soon as possible. As soon as we get orders from the doctor after surgery." She paused momentarily as if she were considering her next words. "We were surprised when he left the hospital so suddenly. We always consult with the family about how to care for burns before they leave, but we didn't get to do that with him." I detected an edge in her voice as if some protocol had been breeched. "Well," she said as she rose, "I'm going to go find him a toy so we can start him flexing his fingers and hands. Did you give him his pain medicine? He needs to have it before he comes."

"Yes," I replied, fearing what her question implied.

She retrieved several toys from the shelf and sat on the platform beside Baby B and me. She held each toy up in front of him and guided his hands to touch it. He had to be taught how to play again. Medical records indicated that at the time of his injury, Baby B was developing normally. At nine months, he was able to sit alone, reach and grasp objects, and pull himself to a standing position on sturdy little legs. But the confidence and physical prowess that had once allowed him to master those initial skills had disappeared. Even the most basic infant actions like lifting his head or rolling over from a lying position had to be relearned after weeks in a hospital bed.

Just before the session ended, Claire pulled out a rotating red musical ball. She took one of Baby B's hands and placed it atop the ball, and together they moved it slowly downward. With each turn, the ball emitted a lovely melody that seemed to mesmerize him. He slipped his arms around the ball and laid his ear against it as if trying to wrap the sweet songs around his soul.

After therapy we escaped back to the house where I crashed on the couch, Baby B beside me in his cradle seat. We stared at one another. I saw in his eyes a reflection of my own dejection, suffocated by events and unable to give voice to them. At that moment I understood completely his binding silence. The blinds were down, rendering a twilight veil over the room, our private hideaway. Our eyes closed simultaneously.

Friday finally arrived. I outsmarted the hydraulic door to PT (I was starting to personify inanimate objects), signed in, sat down, and waited for Claire. Baby B and I were the only ones in the waiting room, Friday being a light day for clinics. A few minutes later, the door opened and a man held it back, as three children entered. All of the children were wearing burn wardrobe: full body suits to protect the skin and flatten scars, and splints on their hands and feet. Little tufts of hair peeked out from their caps. One child wore a facial mold with hollowed-out openings for the eyes, nose, and mouth. The mold pressed against facial skin to minimize scarring. All had hand splints and bandages on their hands and feet. Each child walked with the concentrated gait of a limb injury.

The waiting room was a small enclosure, seven plastic chairs lined against a wall. The children sat down and began quietly talking among themselves while their father signed them in. Waiting rooms are like elevators. There are people who work hard to hide in plain view, avoiding eye contact and verbal interaction. Others open up like elevator doors, pouring their stories out.

In that small place, avoiding one another was impossible. Ben was a big lumberjack of a man with a kind face. We glanced at one another as he took a seat beside his children, breathing heavily.

"Looks like you've got your hands full," I said.

"Yeah, it's been rough." He leaned over, placing his elbows on his knees and rubbed his hands together. "My wife's in the hospital too. I've been going back and forth. Seen enough of hospitals, that's for sure."

"How's she doing?" I asked.

In a low monotone voice, as if he were trying to sort out the details for himself, his story began to unfold. He and his wife had been separated for several months. Every Saturday he went to pick up their children for a weekend visit. One Friday night he got a call that his children and wife had been seriously injured in an explosion. His wife said that after their regular evening pizza dinner, she and the kids had settled on the couch for a night of television watching. She didn't remember anything after that. Emergency personnel told him the propane tank next to their trailer had exploded. Ben said his wife was still in the hospital. He blamed himself. "If I'd been there, I'd have noticed something," he said.

"Maybe," I replied. "But if you had been there then, you might not be here now to help them through this." He stopped rubbing his hands and clasped them together as if he were trying to hold on to that thought.

One week bled into another. I became adept at applying a tourniquet to any emotional flow that threatened to hinder my ability to fulfill the daily responsibilities demanded of me. I operated on autopilot. When PT sessions ended, I gathered Baby B back to me and raced back to the hushed stillness of the house, where we both surrendered to the sweet drug of sleep.

I lived for the weekends, when I was free from the schedules and the directives of others and Lawrence arrived from Austin. By the time he arrived on Friday nights, Baby B and I had bounced back to life from our restorative naps, and I was eager for adult conversation. On those evenings I waited on the couch with Baby B, the murmur of the television shielding the silence until the sound of the key tumbling the door lock grabbed our attention. Baby B leaned forward as I peered over his head. We were as poised for my husband's entrance as a snake for a flute sonata.

It was as if he arrived bringing the other half of me. I felt something shift into place, like the delicate mechanism in a piece of machinery. Everything about our long relationship—

familiarity, connection, comfort—that I had taken for granted, I now viewed through a new threshold.

"Hey, babe." Lawrence stepped through the door, grasping a gym bag, his laptop hanging from a shoulder strap. "The surf's pounding all the way to the seawall. That means there'll be lots of shells and sea glass tomorrow. We'll get an early start."

Through the open door, I could hear the night surf pounding the shore. Lately I had become immune to the sights, sounds, and smells of the sea, even though the Gulf was only a block away. It was as if I wore horse blinders, binding my attention to the road ahead. But Lawrence did far more than lead me back to the beach on weekends. He forged a special connection to Baby B with hands-on participation in his care. During the day, he held, fed, and entertained Baby B. When he cried out in the night, Lawrence went to comfort him.

* * *

By mid-September, everyone's rugged routines were firmly established. Lawrence arrived in Galveston on Fridays; Kanika cycled herself between the hospital and house, treating patients and helping me with Baby B. At times, she and I sounded like a married couple, sparring about which of us worked harder, the stay-at-home mom or the go-to-work doctor. It didn't help that Baby B began sleeping less and less through the night, rarely more than one or two hours before the night terrors began. If I held him, he screamed louder, his body rigid as a rod. Prescribed medications for pain and anxiety had little or no effect.

Kanika and I took him to a consultation with the Shriners psychologist. The psychologist listened to my exasperated accounts of the hellish nights without comment. She nodded and scribbled copious notes on her yellow legal pad. Finally she stuck a period to the last word and leaned back. I leaned forward, anxious for the answer.

She looked at Baby B sitting in his stroller, observant and complacent. "He's coming out of a rough situation. We can't prescribe any more medication for him. Sounds like you'll just have to ride it out. Check back with us in a couple of weeks if things don't improve."

I waited for more. *That's it?* But the psychologist merely returned my stare with silence. And so we returned to the house to "ride it out" until we were worn out. We tried soothing music, leaving lights on, leavings lights off. We bought a rotating disco light that swept the walls with rainbow colors. We wept for him and for ourselves. I tried as best as I could to shield my daughter from the nightly turmoil, concerned that she was not getting the rest she needed on the few precious nights she was home from the hospital.

Even when Baby B's wails were not sailing through the rooms, I could hear Kanika returning calls to the hospital. "This is Dr. Bowen. You paged me. . . . When did the temperature spike? How long since the last injection? Give her . . ."

To drown out the dissonance swirling around me, I turned on late-night radio talk of extraterrestrial signals, sightings, and out-of-body experiences. Drifting off, I could hear the *beep-beep* coming from Kanika's pager.

One day while leafing through Kanika's medical journals I came across an article entitled "ICU Psychosis." It reported that people who spend an extended amount of time in intensive care, where the disappearance of day and night combined with the constant sleep disruption and the ingestion of potent mind-altering drugs wreak havoc on the mind, often experience a state of utter confusion. That article combined with what I knew about Baby B's traumatizing history and hospitalization gave me added insight into his evolving emotional state. Unfortunately, much of what I learned about childhood abuse and its post-traumatic effects were a result of my own research and tenacity and not from any meetings with medical professionals.

I clung to the hope that time, patience, and love would be the keys to easing both Baby B's physical pain and mental anguish.

CHAPTER 18

Gathering Storms

"Clouds, leaves, soil, and wind, all offer themselves as signals of things in the weather. However, not all the storms of life can be predicted."
—*David Peterson*

"I CALLED TO TELL you it's not just a rumor anymore; they're evacuating patients from the hospital," Kanika said. It was Tuesday morning, September 20. Reports of a massive hurricane hurtling toward Galveston had been circulating for several days. Inhabitants along the coast heard these dire predictions every hurricane season. Weather forecasters waved their arms at computerized psychedelic maps as if they were conducting a symphony and reminded everyone that the month marked the 105th anniversary of the 1900 Galveston hurricane that killed eight thousand people. Some people muted the television or went for a bathroom break. Some secured their storm shutters. Others boarded windows with plywood. Hardly anyone actually left the island.

"Hold on; let me take a quick look outside," I said. The sun cast egg yolk yellow streaks across the blue sky. Fluffy white animal-shaped clouds crawled by. Across the street, our elderly neighbor, Mr. Thompson, sat serenely on his porch as he did every day until the midday sun, spreading like slow-melting butter, heating up, before heading inside. The grandmother next door emerged from her van with a load of groceries and an army of grandchildren. A runner jogged past with her dog trotting briskly beside her.

"It doesn't look like anybody else is preparing to leave," I said.

"We're the first to be notified," Kanika said. "If they're making preparations to evacuate patients, we need to start packing too. But keep your appointment with PT. They'll want to give you last-minute instructions. . . . I've got to go. I'm being paged. I don't know when I'll be home. I've got a meeting later about the evacuation. Start thinking about what we want to take."

I hung up the phone, stepped out, and looked up at the clear blue sky. Strangely, not a single seagull or pelican soared above.

Mr. Thompson spotted me and waved. "Gonna be a beautiful day," he shouted.

"Sure is," I replied. Initially, Kanika's neighbors viewed me with a mixture of curiosity and skepticism. The island was much like a small town when strangers moved onto the street— speculation spread.

"We heard something about a sick baby and you coming to help out," someone had commented. I imagined what they really wanted to say was, "*Why would you leave your husband and move in with your daughter to care for a sick child who isn't even related?*" No doubt they thought there was more to the story. However, as they watched Lawrence arrive and depart on a regular basis, I became a little less of a question mark. It appeared that his continual reappearance lent credence to my story.

I went back inside and stood, surveying the room. Propped

up in the center—surrounded by pillows, blankets, and toys—
Baby B looked up at me with wide brown eyes and arched his
brows. "Don't worry; we're taking your toys." It was not fair that
he should have to flee, once again stripped of everything. "But
right now we have to get to physical therapy."

As soon as we arrived, we were directed to the treatment
room instead of the rehab area. The treatment room occupied
a small, drab corner space. Shelves were jam-packed with jars,
tubes, bottles, and bandages. Exotic instruments—miniature
buzz saws, drills, and assorted cutting implements—littered the
countertops.

Master craftsmen in the area of burn paraphernalia, the
physical therapists created casts and plastic molds to aid in
minimizing the effects of burn injury. An independent subgroup
of the hospital hierarchy, they had the primary responsibility for
post-surgical rehabilitation. They took pride in performing their
duties with limited directives from the doctors. Chief among
those duties was to teach parents and caretakers complicated
burn care management. With both adults and children
packed into the room, no space existed for privacy curtains or
partitions so parents tried to provide nurturing shields while
performing the procedures that were required to heal their
child. The children were amazingly stoic and composed. There
was rarely any stronger reaction to the pain than wincing or
muted weeping. I'd seen far more emotional displays in the
grocery line from a child denied gum. Still, a pervasive sense of
sadness permeated the room, as dense and heavy as the evening
fog that crept in from the sea.

As we passed into the treatment area, I noticed that the rehab
room was empty. Usually at that hour, patients and therapists
were well into their routines. Claire turned and greeted us as we
walked in. "Hey," she said. "Be with you in a sec. Have a seat."
She was giving instructions to a woman who looked confused

and upset. Claire spoke a mixture of Spanish and English to her. "*No va hoy. Manana, manana.*"

"*Pero, donde, donde?*" asked the woman.

"At McDonald House. *Comprende?* Understand?"

"*Si, si,*" said the woman. "*Gracias.*" She took her son's hand and walked out, her face filled with anxiety.

The majority of children treated at Shriners in Galveston were from Latin American countries. Usually more than one sibling suffered injuries, and the burns tended to be severe, encompassing the entire body because the fires usually began in small wooden houses that ignited quickly and imploded inward. Candles and cooking fires were often the culprits.

I sat down with Baby B on my lap, and cupped his bandaged hands in mine, palms turned upward as we were taught. Claire sat facing us and began uncoiling the layers of bandages and gauze. He watched intently—the interplay of her hands with his.

"It's hard for them when they don't know what's happening," she said.

"Yes," I said. "Maybe that's why he's always watching, trying to figure it out."

"Oh no, I mean our families who don't speak English," said Claire. "I was trying to explain to the woman who just left that we would pick her and her son up at McDonald House for the evacuation tomorrow. So are you all packed and ready to go?"

"Not yet. I'm still trying to decide what to take. How about you?" I asked.

"A group of us will form a caravan with patient families to a safe area early in the morning to get ahead of the traffic." Claire, calm and confident as ever, often said she regarded caring for children as much a calling as a profession. "Is Kanika leaving with you?" she asked.

"As soon as she can get away from the hospital tomorrow."

Claire rewrapped Baby B's hands and gave me a few additional instructions about wound care and an extra supply of bandages.

"Just keep doing what you've been doing," she said. "You're lucky; you'll have Kanika there if you have any problems."

We wished each other good luck and a safe trip through the coming storm, and I hurried on to my next stop, the pharmacy. We had no idea how long we would be away from Shriners. If the hurricane hit the island as a Category 5 as forecasters predicted, we could be gone indefinitely. I had to make sure Baby B had an adequate supply of medications and materials for our stay in Austin.

I parked the stroller next to the Dutch door and waited for Emily, who reminded me of the Breck Girl commercial, blond hair and a sunshiny smile. She walked over and leaned out of the half-door and looked at Baby B.

"How's he doing today?" she asked. Like the other pharmacists, Emily seemed to take a personal interest in each child. They were always happy to see a child who had initially come in clinging to life coming back and thriving. At that time, medications, like every other service, was free of charge to outpatients. Patient families were never asked for an insurance card or sent a single bill. The hospital's motto, "Once a Shriners' kid, always a Shriners' kid," reflected a no-boundaries spirit to helping children.

"He's getting better every day," I said, handing her my list. "I just need to make sure we have enough meds before we leave."

She took the list and returned with a bulging paper bag. "I put some cream in there that parents say helps the kids with the itching," she said, handing me the bag. "Are you and Kanika leaving together?"

"Yep, tomorrow." I replied. "Thanks for everything." I pushed the stroller into the elevator and hurried back to pack.

* * *

I paused for the stoplight at the corner of 14st and Broadway Avenue, Galveston's main thoroughfare. To my left, the rebuilt historic Sacred Heart Catholic Church loomed majestic with its bright white exterior gleaming in the midday sun. The original Sacred Heart was swept into the sea in the Great Storm like thousands of other buildings. I watched a woman in a halter top, shorts, and flip-flops mount the steep steps of the church and disappear through its ornate wooden door.

On the right, the grandiose Bishop's Palace, built of Texas limestone and surrounded by a wrought-iron fence, maintained its superiority over other historic mansions lining Broadway as one of the few buildings to survive the hurricane of 1908. Originally a private residence known as the Gresham House belonging to a politician-turned-lobbyist, it was purchased by the Catholic Diocese for the bishop and dedicated as a museum after his death. People strolled leisurely around it, taking pictures and peering through the gate.

Along the grassy divider on Broadway, rows of poisonous oleander shrubs splayed clusters of white and pink flowers beneath behemoth palm trees. Layers of fronds hung limp and lifeless from the crown of the trees, cooked dry brown by the August heat.

Cars crawled up and down Broadway at their usual plodding pace. Drivers were not hunched over the steering wheel, wild-eyed speeding through the streets, plowing into other cars like some Hollywood movie of the week, trying to escape the impending hurricane.

As I pulled in front of the house, I looked to see if people were loading their cars, preparing to leave, but not a soul was in sight.

Across the street, the heat had already driven Mr. Thompson from his perch on the porch. At the house next to his, a large corner residence restored in the Victorian architectural style with magenta bougainvillea climbing up and trailing across the second floor balcony, someone stood snapping pictures.

Several motorists passed, music drifting from their cars. I wondered if radio programs were being interrupted by updates about the storm, and if the drivers, like me, observed the clear cerulean sky and thought *false alarm*. I might have spent the rest of my day in the same state of denial if I hadn't just come from the hospital where evacuation preparations were already underway.

Since I had never unpacked my suitcase and simply retrieved and replaced items on a day-to-day basis, my biggest challenge was to make sure that Baby B had everything he needed until we could return to Shriners. But how long would that be? A hurricane of the magnitude predicted would devastate the island. Our little house was only a block from the beach. Even if Shriners managed to escape major damage and remain in operation, where would we stay while he received therapy if the house was destroyed? Instead of making lists and preparations to leave, I lay down beside Baby B and watched sleep settle on his sweet, soft face. I gradually drifted off also as a whirlpool of "what ifs" swirled through my mind like an eddy at the edge of the seashore.

Nicole called later that afternoon, and we talked about the plan to leave the next day.

"What time will you be home?" she asked.

"I'm not sure what Kanika has to do at the hospital tomorrow, but we'll probably leave around noon, which should get us home between five and six o'clock."

"Call me when you get there, and I'll come right over," she said.

Next, I called my son in Dallas. We hadn't talked in quite a while, and I wanted to bring him up to date on the approaching storm and our return to Austin.

"Is Dad going up to help you pack and get out?" he asked.

"We'll talk tonight," I replied. "I don't think that would make much sense, though; it just means we would have three cars on the road trying to stay together instead of two. I'll call you when we get to Austin."

* * *

Kanika arrived home from the hospital late and left again to fill both vehicles with gas. Living a minimalist beach lifestyle enabled us to pack our things quickly. The bulk of what we loaded into the vehicles belonged to Baby B. Anyone who has travelled with small children knows that they can accumulate enough equipment to require a caravan of camels. Luckily for us, for the first time in weeks, Baby B slept through that entire night.

By the next morning, Wednesday, September 21, Hurricane Rita had raced from a tropical storm to a Category 5 hurricane. Officials, mindful of the mistakes made during Hurricane Katrina three weeks earlier, issued a mandatory evacuation order. My husband called that morning from work to ask when we would be leaving.

"We're all packed except for things that can't go in until the last minute," I said.

"You need to leave pretty soon. You don't want to be on the road after dark," he said.

I agreed with him that that was our goal, and we would make it.

We finished talking, and I returned to the bedroom to help Kanika finish Baby B's bath treatment.

"Your dad is worried about us getting home before dark."

"You know dad; he's a worrywart. We will. I've got to go back to the hospital for a few minutes. The nurses can't convince this sweet old guy I've been taking care of to be evacuated to a nursing home."

"What are you going to do?" I asked. "Bundle him up, bring him back, and strap him in the seat next to Baby B?"

"Funny, Mom. I'm just going to try to convince him that the nursing home is the best place for him right now and tell him he can come back after the storm if things don't work out."

After Kanika left, I used my nervous energy to crisscross the house, knowing that whatever we left behind would probably not be there whenever we returned. Baby B, looking alert and content after a full night's sleep, sat in his carrier, following my movements like a curious cat. Once again, he was being uprooted, facing a forced evacuation. This time, however, he would not be lifted out under the whirring blades of a helicopter. No shrill sirens would broadcast his departure. Today he would leave without fanfare along with thousands of others. Today he would flee with me, home to my family.

* * *

"Okay, we can leave now." Kanika came through the door, looking cheerful and energized.

"Well, did you convince him to go to a nursing home?" I asked.

"Oh, he kept wavering back and forth. He's afraid once they place him there, they won't let him come out, but he has to go. You ready?"

"Yep, everything's packed, Baby B's been fed, just had the last of his meds, and hasn't napped yet, so hopefully he'll sleep most of the way."

I ran out and started the engine so that the interior of the vehicle would be cool for Baby B, then watched as Kanika exited the bungalow with him. She kissed his forehead, pulled a blanket over his face to protect it from the searing sun, and carried him past the same flowering Esperanza that had greeted him coming in. After she buckled him into my vehicle, I watched her walk to her car and slide behind the wheel. Just before I pulled away from the curb behind her, I looked into my rearview mirror. Baby B looked straight ahead, smiling.

CHAPTER 19

Running from Rita

"I can hear your whisper and distant mutter. I can smell your damp on the breeze and in the sky. I see the halo of your violence. Storm I know you are coming."
— *Robert Fanney*

I TURNED ONTO BROADWAY Boulevard and drove past storied mansions with spacious, manicured yards and verandahs wrapping around them like an embrace. Brass plaques proclaimed the property's proud heritage and history. These mansions shared the same block with weedy, empty lots, decrepit gas stations, strip malls, and struggling storefront businesses. Old Victorian houses, once stately single-family dwellings, now housed antique shops and law offices. More than any other place on the island, Broadway is a testament to Galveston's grandiose past and its precarious present and future.

As I stopped behind Kanika's car at the red light, I observed lines of cars snaking out onto the street from the last gas station before the I-45 entrance. It was a multiplex station with rows of gas pumps, every one occupied. People stood outside their cars, doors thrown open, revealing insides packed with possessions, children, and pets. Some people paced back and forth. Others stood like statues, legs apart, arms folded across their chest, staring at the pumps with a fierce determination. Groups entered and exited the convenience store, carrying bulging plastic bags.

The light turned green, and I followed Kanika onto the I-45 overpass, thankful that she had filled both cars with gas the night before and we were getting out ahead of the crowd. The dashboard clock read 2:15. No doubt, it would take longer than the usual four hours with two cars, and we might have to stop if Baby B became agitated or needed changing. But if we were lucky, the motion of the car would entice him to sleep most of the way. I glanced in the rearview mirror again. Already his eyes had that glazed, vacant stare, signaling sleep.

I turned on the radio and searched for some innocuous music or program that would help keep me alert and concentrated on keeping the distance to Kanika's vehicle close enough that another car could not squeeze in. No matter what, we had to stay connected all the way to Austin. Our strength and safety depended on our not getting separated. Although an occasional vehicle managed to jump between us, I was still able to spot her red car. Traffic moved along at a steady clip. The bay spread out, indenting the shoreline on each side of the elevated highway. Clustered bayside communities with names like Tiki Island dotted the landscape. The houses, built on stilts to withstand flooding, seemed a flimsy defense against the hurricane.

I trailed Kanika onto the Galveston Bridge. It was hard to believe barely a month had passed since I had crossed this bridge to begin my temporary stay with her and Baby B in Galveston. Then, I was approaching the unknown. Now I was fleeing the unknown. Looking skyward I noted again the absence of birds.

We left the bridge, moving with the steady flow of traffic for several miles before it began slowing. Nothing out of the ordinary, considering it was late afternoon. People with construction and service jobs on the island who lived on the mainland generally arrived early for work and left early to avoid the evening juggernaut. It hadn't occurred to me that the people in the surrounding coastal communities of La Marque, Dickerson, League City, Texas City, and other enclaves dotting the route might also be evacuating until I saw long lines of cars entering the interstate.

Traffic went from slow to stop and go. The digital clock flashed 2:30. It was way too early for it to be that congested. Usually cars didn't start backing up until the I-10 going through Houston.

Baby B had fallen asleep, the vibrating movement of the vehicle delivering him into a deep slumber. During days when he was tired and anxious, fighting a nap, I would drive to where the bay met the end of East Beach, turn off the engine, and watch the sleek cargo ships skimming through the waters as graceful as swans. "See those big ships, Baby B? Where are they going?" He would gaze at the ships from his lofty perch in the back as if he might actually be considering the question. By the time we returned to the house, he was sound asleep.

I snapped back to the present to see Kanika's right rear signal light blinking. I inched up close enough behind to merge to the next lane with her. *We have to stay together! Stay asleep until we get past this, Baby B, please. Traffic will thin out soon. It's probably just a fender bender. Someone driving too close. Somebody on the phone, not paying attention. Rubberneckers, gawking at nothing.*

But as I looked out over the rows of static cars, it became clear this was no ordinary traffic jam. Splayed out across the lanes loomed controlled chaos, a virtual interstate parking lot. Vehicles darted back and forth like sanderlings, but never advanced.

Paralleling the interstate were block after block of serial

strip malls, big box stores, and fast food chains, a cornucopia of civilization and its trappings. The blazing summer sun streamed down and reflected off the procession of chrome and steel. People were sealed inside their cars with windows closed tight against the vapors and heat. However, in some vehicles, faces glistening with sweat hung out windows. What would happen if my vehicle overheated? Without air conditioning, stranded on the interstate desert, wrapped in bandages, Baby B's body temperature would quickly rise to dangerous levels. I pushed the possibility from my mind. *Bad enough without imagining the worst.*

Two hours later Kanika's right blinker flashed. We were approaching the Sam Houston Tollway turn-off. Normally, getting to I-40 took only thirty minutes. I activated my blinker and edged over, leaving just enough room for her to cross in front of me. For now, it seemed that drivers had settled into stalled traffic. Blocking someone else would not get them out. Moreover, no one wanted the added aggravation of a fender bender without any police presence.

The Houston Tollway is an expansive, monotonous stretch of interstate. Toll booth payment is required for the privilege of avoiding side roads and traffic lights.

Kanika and I joined the procession of vehicles pressing forward. *Once we've rounded the bend, things will open up.* I followed as she inched forward, crossing four lanes. Although temporarily separated, I managed to keep her in sight.

As I scanned the road ahead, the sea of cars, coiling endlessly into the distance, came into view. My heart sank as I realized there would be no lanes opening up, no surge forward. We would fade to black like a *Twilight Zone* episode where people suddenly realize that they are stuck on an eternal highway, encased in vehicles destined to be their final tombs.

For the next hour, traffic chugged along like a faulty conveyor belt. From the rearview mirror, I saw Baby B shifting in his seat. He had slept for more than three hours. He needed food and medication and changing. I flicked my flasher, a signal to Kanika that we needed to exit. We began our leapfrog dance toward the exit and squeezed into the turn-off lane, where we joined cars at a standstill. We had been idling in the same spot for over thirty minutes when Kanika put on her emergency blinkers and moved off the road to the shoulder. I punched my emergency signal and followed her past the glaring stares of motorists who thought we were attempting to cut the line.

I hoped Kanika knew where she was going because we would never be allowed back into the stream if the shoulder became blocked for some reason. Soon the crossroad came into view, and I relaxed. I followed her off the interstate and down the outer road for several miles. Not many cars were on the outer roads, and for good reason. These roads sometimes veered away from the interstate. One could easily take a wrong turn and end up in the middle of a cornfield or grass as brown and shriveled as shredded wheat. Weathered mobile homes lurked behind the dense foliage of overgrown fields where kudzu vine spread like wildfire, snatching and snaring dwellings, shrouding them in a thick green fortress.

We passed a gated community of McMansions. The houses peeked out from behind a stockade of brick walls and iron gates built to halt encroachments of any kind. A mile later, we spotted a service station. We hadn't covered enough miles to need gas, but the station had a small convenience store and restrooms. I pulled up beside Kanika in the parking lot.

"We'll be over there in the shade," I said, pointing to a large oak tree in the corner of the lot.

I parked under the canopy of the tree and climbed into the backseat so that I could change Baby B's diaper, which was a major feat given that the car seat was the size of a throne.

Lethargic and fretful, he sank into my lap like a sack of potatoes as I made a cursory examination of his bandages.

"Hey, Mom. I could hardly see you squeezed up between that seat."

"Did you think I'd taken off, hitchhiking to Austin?"

"The way things are going, you might get there a lot faster."

"No kidding. How are the restrooms?" I asked.

"Don't ask. Try not to look."

I walked past a cashier whose back was turned as he stood glued in spot, listening to the weather report on a portable television on the counter. In an excited pitch, the forecaster laid out the path of the hurricane, encouraging everyone to follow the evacuation plans, get out of town, and be prepared for packed highways. I wondered if the cashier was calculating the risk of remaining. I imagined him leaving the store, walking down the road to his house, closing the door, and taking his chances at home. Looking at the clogged interstate in the distance as I hurried toward the car, it seemed as good of a bet as any.

Kanika was wiping Baby B's face with a cool, wet cloth when I returned. "He seems kind of out of it," I said.

"Yeah," she replied. "That's because after he's had his meds, we usually have him up and moving. Now they just make him lethargic."

"Did he eat anything?"

"Not much, but he drank a lot. As long as we can keep him hydrated and cool, he'll be okay."

As long as the air conditioning keeps going. As long as the car keeps going. As long as I keep going.

"Let's get going," I said. "Traffic will start moving once we veer off to the I-10 flyover into Houston. I'm hoping a lot of people are heading for San Antonio."

Kanika strapped Baby B back in and walked over to her car, and we each snapped on our signalers and squeezed our way back onto the Sam Houston interstate. An hour later we inched around the bend toward I-10 into six lanes of endless traffic. To the right, jutting into the sky, a giant waterslide structure of steel and concrete held cars suspended hundreds of feet up in the air like a stalled ferris wheel. Eventually, we ascended the same flyover and waited hundreds of feet up in the air, suspended in purgatory between heaven and hell, for the traffic to advance. Shifting cumulus clouds drifted through the big, blue Texas sky, the shapes morphing into spaceships and the fantastical. The September sun was cresting, enveloping and heating up the car's interior. I adjusted the air and vents for maximum output, lowered the visor, and shielded my eyes with my hand to block the sun's glare. Even though it was technically fall, the Texas temperature still simmered.

I squinted to get a better view of vehicles stretching across every lane into infinity. The calamity would continue. Having obeyed the mandatory evacuation order, masses of people were already on I-10. We descended the flyover, landed on the I-10 airstrip cutting through Houston, and grounded on the interstate tarmac. Cars dotted the off-road pavement, hoods yawning wide. Families stood outside their vehicles in the sweltering heat, looking dismayed and bewildered. Radio briefs reported that cars were running out of gas, engines overheating, and tires deflating. Some people, seeing what lay ahead, reported they were returning home rather than risk getting swept away by the hurricane sitting on the interstate.

The cell phone rang. "Where are you now?" Lawrence asked.

"Stuck on I-10." I gave him a brief description of the last few hours.

"Are the eastbound lanes open?" he asked. "Maybe I could get to you."

"Don't even think about it!" I said. "The only things going

that way are rescue vehicles. Even if we ended up on the side of
the road, you couldn't get to us. I don't need to be worried about
you in addition to all that's happening. We'll be okay. Kanika
and I are sticking together. Nothing is going to happen."
  "Okay," he said. "Okay. I guess you're right. I'll check back
later. Be careful. Love you."

*　*　*

By 8 p.m. dusk was fading to dark. We had been on the roadways
for six hours. My cell phone rang again. "We're getting near
Katy," Kanika said. "It's the last town before a long stretch of
nothing. Doesn't look like things are going to move any faster.
If we don't get off now we'll be stuck on this freeway all night."
  "I agree. Baby B looks pretty depleted."
  "Okay," she said. "Follow me."
  We maneuvered our way to the Katy exit lane. Pitch dark
dropped like stage drapes. Others must have decided Katy
was a good place to get off the highway treadmill because exit
lanes were jammed. The earlier goodwill of fellow travelers had
evaporated. Cars closed ranks quickly to prevent others from
slipping into the lane. I don't know how we managed to move
over to the exit except that my fear of our getting separated
outweighed any caution I would have ordinarily exhibited.
  We languished on the outer road, surrounded by weedy
rural fields. The country dark was complete except for white
headlights and red taillights of thousands of cars. Ahead a
stop sign prevented cars from exiting the freeway quickly and,
because crossing traffic had no stop sign, the results were near
accidents, repeated horn blasts, and backups in both directions.
We could have sat there half the night had Kanika not activated
her emergency flashers and pulled to the right onto the shoulder
of the road. I punched my flashers and darted behind her. But
as she eased forward, a farm truck pulling a cow trailer swung

to the right onto the shoulder, blocking our way. Each time the driver saw Kanika attempting to pass, he moved his rig farther to the right.

I watched helplessly as they played cat and mouse, each swinging farther out onto the shoulder as she attempted to go around him, my heart pounding. We were on an outer road on the outskirts of nowhere. Except for the coruscating car lights, it was as dark as a bat cave. What if this person got worked up enough to explode out of the truck and up to my daughter's car? What if he tried to force his way into her car? Even though thousands of people were on the road, I was sure no one would leave the safety of their car to help us. I began blowing my horn, long and hard. I hoped that the noise would remind him that other people were present to witness anything he might be thinking of doing.

I don't know if Kanika interpreted my blowing the horn as my wanting her to move ahead or if she decided that enough was enough, but when he swung his trailer out to block her for the third time, she gunned her engine, skidded around him halfway off the shoulder and onto the field, and sped ahead. I raced behind her, hoping to get between her and the truck without losing sight of her in the enveloping darkness. We drove crazily, half on the shoulder and half off. I was confident my SUV could tackle the terrain, but her car was a compact, low to the ground. If she ran into a gutter, hit a rock or road debris, things could deteriorate dangerously. We kept going, our lights flashing, tires grinding and skidding, charging ahead before anyone else could divide us, my adrenaline pumping.

Desperation set in. Baby B had been strapped inside his car seat for hours. He was too quiet, too still. He needed to be unseated, held close and comforted. Every hour he was confined mimicked the weeks he was bound to a hospital bed. All the weeks we had worked to stimulate his senses back to awareness were slowly slipping away in that terrible trek across Texas.

We eventually made it through the underpass to the other side of the expressway to the parking lot of a chain hotel. The lot was full of vehicles of every make and model: campers, semis, motorcycles saddled with bulging black plastic bags, cars with boxes and clothes pressed against the windshields. We drove to the drop-off area, and I waited behind Kanika's car while she went to check in. I took a long look at Baby B. He was sallow and glassy eyed. It seemed he had receded inside himself. Perhaps survival necessitated that he temporarily withdraw like a turtle retreating into its shell so that danger passed over and around. I hoped he would reemerge, when it was safe.

*   *   *

I watched as Kanika emerged from the hotel doors with the same distracted, determined look that had become part of her lexicon.

"We lucked out," she said. "Got the last room."

"Thank God," I replied. Inside the hotel lobby, people milled around, trading tales about the miserable miles they had spent in traffic. Their words were punctuated with puffs of nervous chuckles and spurts of righteous indignation regarding the bad planning state government had executed in mandating the massive evacuation without a plan to prevent what was taking place.

"Not an emergency vehicle or a cop anywhere," someone said. "Heaven help us if we ever had a national emergency; might as well stay home and wait for the bombs to fall," another voice interjected.

"What are we paying all this money in toll and highway taxes for if we might as well be driving on a two-lane road?" cried a woman holding an infant as she tried to chase down a toddler.

We made a beeline straight for our room. Luckily it was on the first floor. I was in no mood to wait for an elevator or ride up in one, having to listen to people's complaints. Even though I was in full agreement with their sentiments, I preferred to suffer in silence.

The good thing about hotel chains is their predictability, providing a quiet, clean cocoon in which to collapse. I laid Baby B on one of the beds, and Kanika and I performed our routine examination of his body. We gave him meds and coaxed him to drink. After he drifted off, I slipped over to the window and looked out. It was nearing 11 p.m., and across the parking lot on I-10 a chain of cars formed a link of lights. *The last room. We could still be in that streaming mass.*

At four the next morning, Kanika clicked on the bedside lamp. "Traffic should have thinned out by now. We'd better get on the road before it starts stacking up again." I saw her across the room in the predawn and once again envied her ability to sprint into action.

I groaned and looked over at Baby B sleeping peacefully. Then half rolling, half stumbling out of bed, I shuffled over to the window and peeped through the heavy curtains like a spying neighbor. The multitude of people and cars from which we had extricated ourselves hours ago remained. *Welcome back. We've been waiting for you!*

The room receipt had already been placed outside the door. Baby B remained asleep, freeing us to make the leap from hotel to car in one swift sweep. Within a matter of minutes, we left the parking lot and wedged our way into the stop-and-go traffic. Gray dawn slowly pushed out the dark night. The sun rose to spread its red and yellow embers across the horizon and open fields. Soon it would stoke up the simmering morning heat to a boiling point. Eventually the expressway curved to a highway divided by a grassy median and bordered by vast fields. Cows and horses grazed, unruffled by the passing procession.

Fifty-some miles and five hours after leaving the Katy hotel, at around 9 a.m., we approached the agricultural community of Columbus. A fast food burger restaurant and a busy intersection with streets leading to strip malls and gas stations were in plain view from I-10. Anticipating fuel and food, motorists began merging right toward lanes leading into the town. But cemented in the center of the exit lane like stop signs was an unwelcoming committee of two armed policemen, legs spread in a commanding stance, necks like fireplugs, their faces already scorched red by the early sun. Grinning from ear to ear and bantering with sinister glee, the officers extended their arms in looping theatrical arcs, pointing people past the turn-off.

As they raised their arms, their weapons were visible. Guns jutted out from their substantial girths, and occasionally they rested a hand on their holsters. As I watched their performance, I remembered reports about people seeking escape from Hurricane Katrina being blocked access to certain areas of the city. When we hear those things, we like to believe that were we confronted with similar circumstance, our community—we—would act more compassionately. But when the opportunity arises, we too assume a stance of indifference and self-preservation.

Drivers initially assumed the police were there to help direct traffic into town. But it slowly dawned on them that they were being waved by like a bad smell. A few drivers banged their open palms on their steering wheels in anger. Others looked at the police in disbelief, lifting their hands, palms up. "Why?" Children pressed their faces against windows and cried, as the chance to flee the confines of the car disappeared.

I might have understood if they had held up signs saying, "SORRY, OUT OF WATER," "OUT OF GAS," "OUT OF

HOSPITALITY." But to laugh? Nobody wants to see a cop with a gun riding high on his hip laughing in the face of tragedy. A few miles past Columbus, the overhanging sign announced the Hwy-71W lane to Austin. It loomed like a rainbow's promise. We sailed around the curve, heading home, leaving behind the traffic slogging along I-10 toward San Antonio. I was elated to discover our speed increasing from ten miles per hour to fifty miles an hour. We made a brief stop to refuel in Bastrop and attend to Baby B. At noon, almost twenty-four hours after leaving Galveston, we approached my subdivision. As we passed our neighborhood grocery store, I called Lawrence on my cell. "We're about five minutes away."

"I'm waiting for you," he replied.

The wide street spread open like a warm welcome. During the weeks since I had departed, it was as if time had stood still. Although it was nearing the end of September, people were as sequestered in their houses against the relentless heat as the day I had left in August. As I drove past houses, I thought about the families inside. Were their lives as tidy as their lawns? Children healthy and happy? Were they conscious of the precarious nature of those random gifts?

Kanika turned into our driveway, and I pulled in beside her. I pressed the garage door opener and saw Lawrence's legs sprouting from beneath the door as it lifted. He ducked under the door and caught me up in a hug as I climbed out of my vehicle. "Glad you made it safely," he said.

"Me too," I said, burying my face in his neck.

"Hey, Daddy." My daughter and husband embraced, and I heard them exchange words in their teasing back and forth way before he returned to the SUV, opened the rear door, and peered into the backseat.

"You look like you're ready to get out of there. Time for a change of scenery, right, buddy?"

Baby B shifted his eyes toward Lawrence. Did he recognize the voice?

My husband unbuckled the cradle straps and lifted him out. Kanika and I stood aside, murmuring, "Be careful, watch your step." We marched toward the door in a triumvirate, determined that this fragile life, uprooted again, be transplanted to higher, safer ground.

Lawrence carried Baby B into our home and deeper into our hearts.

CHAPTER 20

Sweet Respite

"Hope has two beautiful daughters. Their names are anger and courage; anger at the way things are, and courage to see that they do not remain the same."
—*St. Augustine*

THAT THURSDAY I watched the evening news as cameras panned the highways, capturing vehicles that remained moored in the bottlenecked lanes we had escaped. "Contraflow lanes have been ordered," read the ticker tape scrolling continuously across the bottom of the screen. Unfortunately, the order was too little and too late for millions. Coordination and implementation of the contraflow plan took up to ten hours. People were still stuck in cars on clogged roadways the next day.

On Friday morning, September 23, time ran out for twenty-three people who were killed when a bus carrying forty-five nursing home evacuees erupted into flames and exploded on Interstate 45. Authorities said the fire started in the brake system, and the passengers' therapeutic oxygen tanks may have caused the bus to explode. Many of the passengers were mobility impaired, making escape difficult or impossible.

The effects of Hurricane Rita on Galveston Island were nowhere near the severity anticipated. Ironically in Texas, more people were killed or injured trying to escape the calamity that never arrived. The feared storm surge struck farther east, as the storm's center came ashore at the Louisiana border. Winds blowing offshore in Texas actually flattened the surge, which at only seven feet was well below the height of the Galveston seawall.

The traffic volume did not ease for nearly forty-eight hours as more than three million residents had evacuated the area in advance of the storm—the largest evacuation in U.S. history.

In the end, Hurricane Rita was the fourth most intense Atlantic hurricane ever recorded and the most intense tropical cyclone ever observed in the Gulf of Mexico. It killed seven people directly, and many others died in evacuations and from indirect effects.

* * *

Grateful to be home, I hunkered down in my foxhole of familiarity and security. Simple pleasures I once took for granted like sitting down to a dinner with my family or lying down in my own bed at the end of a long day and waking up beside my husband took on new dimensions. During mornings, my bare feet settled into soft carpet. The scent of coffee mingled with the smell of home. Life took on a richer, more satisfying texture.

As I sipped coffee in the front room, I watched children run across the street to a waiting school bus. It struck me that school had started while I was away. There was a time when my life was ruled by the school calendar, with vacations, doctor's appointments, and social and family gatherings all revolving around the beginning and ending of its sacred schedule.

The flowerbed next to the fence sprouted weeds beside

summer flowers wilting and going to seed. Their ragged condition reminded me that my fall ritual of turning over and replenishing the soil and planting crocus and daffodil bulbs had passed. Each spring I looked forward to seeing the sturdy little stalks break though, inspired by their ability to fight through the cold, dark crust of winter and break out with a burst of brightness. Would anything emerge this spring?

"Hey, Mom."

Kanika came bouncing down the stairs in pink pajamas. Even though she was in her twenties, she still looked like a teenager. The horrendous hours required for internship and residency had not diminished her youthful exuberance. The years I had spent chauffeuring her to study sessions, band, and cheerleading practice came flooding back. The arguments, the laughs, the growing pains of adolescence and adulthood coalesced in that single moment.

"Hey, Sweetie. You look just like back in high school coming down those stairs. Remember all those mornings I drove you to school because you wouldn't ride the school bus?"

"Yep," she said, laughing. She sat on the couch next to me and for a moment we were silent, looking at the idling bus.

"Remember the time that kid cut you off, and you followed him into the parking lot and gave him a tongue lashing?" she said.

"Yeah, I sure do. Wouldn't do that today—might get shot." She nodded her head in agreement.

"What's it like when you walk into a patient's room? Do they ever say you look too young to be a doctor?"

"Usually they ask me if I'm there to change the sheets or remove the meal tray, even though I'm wearing my white coat, tags, and a stethoscope around my neck."

"And then?" I asked.

"Well, I'll identify myself, explain to them how their

operation is going to unfold, what to expect afterward. When I've finished giving all those details, you know what their next question is?"

"What?"

"When's the doctor coming?"

We looked at each other and burst out laughing.

She said she had grown accustomed to these slights. I thought about the multitude of personalities, both professionals and patients, and the assortment of declining bodies she confronted daily and was amazed by her continued devotion and enthusiasm. I remembered a quote from Eleanor Roosevelt: "No one can make you feel inferior without your consent."

"Why are you up so early?" I asked. "You should catch up on sleep while we're here."

"I've already gotten more sleep than I usually do," she replied. "What about you? You're up too."

"Just trying to get myself some free time before Baby B wakes up."

Although we had lived together in the same cramped space for a month, home in Austin was our first opportunity to have a mother-daughter conversation. It felt wonderful to reestablish that connection. We talked about people and activities that had taken backseat post-Baby B. She had already shared with me that she was in a serious relationship with Alpha, a man she had dated during medical training in another state. I often heard her talking on the phone to him after all of the night commotion had ceased. Although I had yet to meet him, I trusted her judgment when it came to her personal life.

We sat for a few more minutes, each engaged in our own thoughts, and then wandered off to soak up the last slip of silence before the day delivered its demands.

I spied a book of short stories and leafed through it, trying to remember the last one I read. Reading had once been a daily pleasure. I could not have imagined going through an entire day without picking up a book, but I no longer had the time or concentration it required.

I ambled into the kitchen. Several envelopes of winter vegetable seed packets I had purchased on sale were spread on the table. It's said that humans are the only species that can take as much pleasure in preparing for the future as in the moment itself. Nothing seems more representative of that theory than imagining a vegetable garden full of bounty before the first seed is ever placed in the ground.

The table appeared exactly as I had left it. Had my husband even bothered to sit down at the table for a meal? Or did he mirror my bad habit in Galveston of mindlessly grabbing anything to stave off the hunger? I looked at the wall calendar. It was marked with events and places we had planned on attending in the coming months, but all that would be on hold for now.

I looked forward to Nicole's arrival. Not only had she listened to me vent on the telephone, but she had been to Galveston with Lawrence and pitched right in to help with Baby B. A span of six years separated Nicole and Kanika. Always fearlessly independent, Kanika had never bowed to the position of little sister. Although they had different personalities and preferences, they were very much alike in their core beliefs and their willingness to help others. I was confident that as they matured, they would grow to appreciate each other's strengths and develop a strong sisterly bond.

Later that day, I observed the two of them deep in discussion about how best to accomplish a procedure for Baby B that would be the least traumatizing for him. They gave him a bath treatment and laid him on a pad between them. The pad was surrounded by an array of towels, bandages, and creams. They traded ideas back and forth, listening to each other's suggestions with patience and respect, and together decided on a course of action. I smiled, happy to have witnessed the combination of their strengths to serve Baby B.

* * *

I called my son Lawrence Jr., in Dallas, hoping his family might visit before I returned to Galveston. Whenever I spoke with him on the phone, the sound of his voice with the deep baritone of his father's threw me into a time warp of past meeting present. As the firstborn sibling and the only son, he is the recipient, both good and not so good, of that unique position. A six-year span exists between him and sister Nicole, and a twelve-year space between him and sister Kanika. He was an only child for the first six years of our marriage. His sweet temperament and easy disposition were the impetus for my desire for more children. The years with him seemed lightning quick, and his growing up and leaving for college seemed to take place like a fast-forwarded movie. As he spun off into adulthood, my young family was still evolving. In a flash, my son transitioned from a boy to a man to a husband and a father. He raced through all those roles like an NFL quarterback with a football, while his dad, his sisters, and I have cheered him on from the sidelines.

He became a husband and father at a young age and achieved a level of maturity and responsibility when many young males still lived at home. As he drifted away from me into the sea of life, was what I thought a signal for help really a hearty wave good-bye? How does a mother let go when she has been the lifeguard guiding her children away from undertows?

He and I had not discussed my stay in Galveston or my role as Baby B's caretaker. He had not asked me any questions nor expressed any opinion. Although I was curious as to what he thought about the situation, I would have been disappointed and saddened if he were not supportive, so I resisted the temptation to ask. *Don't ask the question if you're not prepared to accept the answer.*

"Hey, Mama."

Caller ID has to be the greatest invention of the century, the element of surprise eliminated.

"Hi, son. How have you been?"

"Great. Lots of things going on with work, kids, the usual. How's it feel to be home?"

"Wonderful. I'm calling to see if you and Kimberly can bring the kids this weekend. I'll probably be going back to Galveston next week and was hoping to see them before leaving."

"Wish we could, but league sports have started and games are scheduled every weekend. They're here now, though. Upstairs, I think. Want to talk to them?"

"Sure I do," I replied, quick and cheerful. The receiver made clatter contact with the counter, and I heard him shout, "Malik, Rashaad, Myah! Nana is on the phone. Come down!" When Kanika was born, I had begun the tradition of African names. My desire for that cultural connection had been conceived in the wake of *Roots* by Alex Haley. My son continued the custom.

I pictured him standing at the stairs. After a pause, he shouted again. I heard background noises mingled with muffled voices and footsteps pounding the stairs like charging horses. The phone was picked up, dropped, and picked up again. Finally, a child's voice broke through. I spoke to each one in an amped-up grandparent voice in an effort to inject a level of excitement into my intrusion. Like most grandparents who are unable to see their grandchildren on a regular basis, I felt a need to overcompensate by being extra gregarious on the phone. I tried hard not to bombard them with a string of generic grandparent questions like "How's school?" "What's your favorite game, toy, or cartoon?" Kids are impatient with the social strain of adult small talk.

"What ya been doin'?" I asked each child as they came on. After the initial "Nothing," I managed to extract a few more words before they handed over the phone to their dad.

"So when you heading back?" he asked.

"Next Sunday. Kanika thinks UTMB will probably have everyone report back to work on Monday." Silence. *Should I reveal more about this sudden shift in my life? What does he think? That I am on an extended vacation with a little charity work thrown in? Why am I so resentful of his seeming lack of interest while at the same time I am reluctant to share the searing experiences of the past month with him?*

*   *   *

The second Sunday after our arrival, Kanika and I once again said our good-byes to Lawrence and Nicole. They watched in the driveway as our cars departed, and I watched them through the rearview mirror, holding my breath and holding back tears as their figures receded.

The chaos that clogged interstate and rural highways had disappeared, and traffic flowed swiftly. After fleeing to temporary arrangements, evacuees had returned to their homes immediately after the announcement that Hurricane Rita had bypassed their area. Therefore, we avoided the mass of people heading home.

We arrived back on Galveston Island without having stopped. Baby B had alternately napped and looked out as the world whizzed by. His eyes fluttered open just as we crossed the Galveston Bridge. We parked in front of the bungalow, and I waited while Kanika unlocked the front door. I thought about Lawrence and I tossing our bags inside, running down the block and across the street where we stood at the seawall, watching as the sun's rays sprayed jewels of twinkling white light across the horizon. Occasionally, leaping dolphins got caught in the flash of a bright eclipse.

I pressed the driver's window down. The salty sea air blew in. The scent was always more aromatic after the Gulf's stagnant waters were swirled and swept clean by storms off the Atlantic. "Well, Baby B, we're back," I said, more to myself than to him. His attention was focused on something outside. Fronds danced wildly at the top of the tall palm trees across the street. "Is that what you're looking at, Baby B? We'll just sit for a minute and watch." A platoon of brown pelicans cut through the crystal clear sky in perfect formation. Unlike their pesky seagull relatives that screeched and careened crazily, the pelicans soared silently overhead in a perfect V.

Although the sky buzzed with activity, the street was deserted. Residents were probably inside their homes enjoying Sunday dinner and relaxing with their families. No doubt they were thankful to have returned to a community still intact. After unloading the car, I called Lawrence to tell him we had arrived safely. Kanika made and took endless calls about patients while I devoted the next few hours to re-acclimating Baby B to the house in the same false cheerfulness I used for my grandchildren.

I had been granted a two-week reprieve, but now I was required to return to serve out the rest of my time. The irony was that I was actually returning to a vacation island—proof that place was less important than state of mind.

After Kanika's calls were completed, we reconvened and cycled into automatic mode with the bath treatments and bedtime rituals that would consume the rest of the evening.

At midnight, I stumbled to bed. I switched on the radio on the bedside table, hoping to drown out thoughts that circled like buzzards as soon as my head hit the pillow. *Had I remembered to secure the bandages with extra surgical tape? Had I remembered to log that last dose of medication? How early in the morning should I wake him for his clinic appointment?* After hours of head static competing with the radio static, I succumbed to a fitful sleep. After raising three children, it had taken me years to be able to sleep through the night. Now once again, that treasured ability was slipping away.

That night the sleep-robbing vampires came back with a vengeance, determined to rob Baby B of his right to lullaby sweet dreams. I heard screams somewhere in my muddled sleep. I tried to will myself to wakefulness, but my limbs remained leaden even as I struggled to detect the source of sound.

I'm back in Galveston.

It wasn't the interruption of sleep that sapped my strength and shrunk my soul . . . it was the knowledge that no matter what I did, he would reject me. He would refuse my offerings of comfort. His body would bow away from my touch and become rigid in my arms. The stiff splints still strapped to his arms pressed hard against my heart. When he looked at me—if he looked at me—his eyes would be filled with terror. The darkness was a heavy hand, pressing me down as I lifted myself and went to him ready for rejection.

The next morning, I pushed Baby B's stroller out of Shriners parking lot onto Market Street, again dodging traffic, and steered us back to the sidewalk, holding my breath through the cigarette smoke coming from huddled hospital employees. Inside the lobby, battered suitcases and bulging duffel bags lined the walls; a splattering of Spanish punctuated the air. Festive could never describe the atmosphere of a hospital that specializes in child burn treatment, but on this particular morning there was an aura of spontaneous good spirits in the air. Even the sober staffers at the check-in desk smiled. The island—and just as important, Shriners—had been spared the ravages of Hurricane Rita.

I signed Baby B in at physical therapy and waited for Claire. PT ran on a strict schedule, and patient families were admonished to be on time. It was not unusual to see a Mexican mother ushering in several children. I thought about the two hours it took me to bathe, bandage, medicate, feed, and transport one child. How in the world did they manage with several? Fortunately, the McDonald House was less than a mile away. People there helped families prepare the children for the day's treatment. In addition, a Shriners van transported them to and from therapies.

"Welcome back," said Claire, smiling broadly and beckoning us into the tiny treatment room. "How'd y'all do?" Claire's soft southern drawl was soothing in the sparse, stark surroundings. Still, I felt that familiar anxiety, anticipating what new hurts she would inflict on Baby B. I sat down in the plastic chair positioned just inside the door with Baby B on my lap.

"Good," I replied, "except for that horrible traffic getting to Austin. A nightmare."

Baby B watched her open and close cabinets and pull supplies from big bins.

"Yes. I heard about the terrible congestion. Fortunately we took our families in the opposite direction farther south, so we missed a lot of that." She pulled up a chair and began to undo the wrapping on Baby B's hand. "I bet you were glad to be in Austin again with your family," she said.

"It was wonderful." If I hadn't wanted to spare her feelings, I could have easily added "but the best part was not having to come here." I had no doubt that every parent who had to bring a child to Shriners was thankful for its generosity and services, but they wished to God they had never had to utilize them.

"How about the families you were with? You stay at a hospital or hotel?"

"Oh no." She laughed. "We stayed in stables."

"Stables?" I asked, incredulous. "What kind of stables?"

"Horse stables. The owners cleaned them out and put down fresh straw and covered it with blankets. We did just fine."

It was hard to imagine. All those children so susceptible to infection and with such fragile skin conditions in stables ... and no air conditioning.

"Wow," I said.

"At night," she continued, "we had glowing lanterns and the women walked around in groups from stall to stall singing to the children. It was very sweet. You have to remember these families are from Mexico. They make do with a lot less."

I was silent. Suddenly, that twenty-four hour crawl to Austin to reach my comfortable home took a backseat to their journey. Claire held Baby B's hands, examining them closely.

"Y'all did a good job with his dressings. Everything looks nice and clean, but it still looks like the contractions are getting worse. I've got a grant for serial casting. I think we'll start doing that next week."

The word "serial" sent out warning signals since it is a word often followed by something sinister: serial rapist, serial murder, serial abuser, and in Baby B's case serial operations.

"You're going to put a cast on his hand?" I asked.

"Uh-huh," she said, nodding. "I'll make a cast to immobilize his hand and fingers. Every three or four days, I'll remove it to check and clean his hand and then apply a new cast. I'm hoping that will keep his hand from contracting more."

More misery.

"You all still see Dr. H in the clinic?" she asked.

"Yes," I replied, still trying to digest "serial casting."

She rewrapped his hands and reapplied the splints. "Okay, I'll see you in a couple of days."

I hurried out and to the elevator. In the lobby, I left Baby B with a kind-looking older woman wearing a uniform and medals identifying her as a member of the Shriners organization. I wanted to spare him the discomfort of being pushed to the parking lot in air as hot and humid as a sauna. I walked with my head down, obsessing about serial casting when BAMM! I walked right into the steel guard lever at the parking entrance. The breath knocked out of me, I pitched backward and almost fell to the ground.

"Are you all right?" asked a woman passing by.

"Yes, thank you," I answered. "My mind was somewhere else."

"I understand. I've been there," she said before turning and walking toward Shriners.

I picked up Baby B and fled from the hospital. I wanted to spend as much time away from serial casting, clinics, appointments, therapists, and doctors as possible. I grabbed a burger from a fast-food drive-through and rushed back to the house. Baby B had fallen asleep, and I managed to carry him inside without waking him. I laid him on a large blue bubble foam pad we had garnered from the hospital and covered it with soft blankets and sheets. We had placed the pad, which looked like a giant Styrofoam cardboard egg container, in the front room so he could observe our coming and going throughout the day. At the hospital, nurses placed the pads on top of mattresses to further cushion the tender, raw flesh of the children. I watched as his wounded body settled into the soft foam, then I plopped down on the floor next to him. I mindlessly gulped down the bland burger, which lodged into the pit of my stomach like a stone, and crawled to the couch and collapsed.

* * *

Kanika called to say she would be at the hospital late. I thought about the long, lonely day stretching into the endless night. In the hours between twilight and nightfall, Baby B would become increasingly agitated, surveying his surroundings as if he were seeing everything, including me, for the first time. A furrow-like pinched piecrust appeared between his eyes.

In reading a book about a woman's husband who had suffered a brain injury, I discovered that this type of disorientation is not uncommon for people who have suffered debilitating trauma. It is sometimes referred to as "sundowning syndrome" and is most often seen in people who are hospitalized "where the abeyance of day and night interferes with the body's circadian rhythms." It confirmed what I had read earlier in a medical journal, that the condition could also be exacerbated by anesthesia and some medications administered for pain and anxiety. Ironically, I recalled that it was also around sundown that Baby B had been scalded.

That evening I decided a walk might do us both good. After his nap, I headed out with Baby B. I stood in front of the house, debating whether to turn left toward the sea or right into the neighborhood. A slight breeze blew in from the Gulf, and the fall day was fragrant with salty air and the scent of foliage bursting with its final fruits. I travelled Galveston's main thoroughfares of 61st, Seawall Boulevard, and Broadway frequently, but the streets surrounding the house were a mystery to me.

I decided to go the opposite direction of the seawall because the breeze coming from the beach would carry sand granules laden with bacteria that could breach Baby B's bandages. Along the way, I made mental notes of our location to keep from getting lost. Side streets are identified by alphabet: Avenue K, Avenue L, Avenue M. Perhaps in the haste to rebuild after disasters, developers had decided that was the most efficient system. It was amusing to follow the alphabet of streets in a *Sesame Street* kind of way.

It was my first foray into my adopted neighborhood. As I pushed Baby B along, I wondered how the sensation of being out in the open air would affect him. I watched him through the mesh at the top of the stroller for any signs of discomfort as we passed small cottages with postage stamp yards mixed amongst grandiose houses surrounded by giant oak, magnolia, and palm trees.

The Galveston Historical Society periodically hired moving crews to haul deteriorating mansions from their original site on the outskirts of Galveston into town. It was an amazing sight to see a multistory Victorian structure hauled through an old neighborhood and positioned on a plot of land. A large sign was then erected, announcing to local residents that the "original elegance" of the structure would be restored in the coming year for the "enrichment of the neighborhood." Locals didn't know what "enrichment" meant since sidewalks remained uninstalled, and the giant aging oak trees that shed leaves and dropped limbs remained untrimmed except when they threatened power lines.

An elderly man, sitting on a porch among rusted appliances and sunken furniture surrounding him like wizened friends, lifted his head like an old tortoise peeking out of its shell. He waved and flashed a wide, toothless grin. Wandering through the quiet tree-lined streets felt like travelling back in time. *Of all places, how did I end up here?*

I periodically paused and bent to peer inside the stroller to see how Baby B reacted to being outdoors. He liked to sit on the porch in the evenings, but other than that we only exposed him to the outdoors when he was transported from vehicle to building. Fortunately he seemed content in the stroller, listening to the breeze whistling through the trees and watching dry leaves roll across the street like giant scurrying beetle bugs.

I wondered how many times in his previous little life he had been taken out for a leisurely stroll along tree-lined streets. It seemed impossible to believe that the same woman who had in a flash so horribly altered his life could have done something as soothing as spending that type of time with him. I thought about how painfully little I knew about his previous baby life. All I knew was what I had read from accounts about that fateful evening she hurt him, and the resulting events that had miraculously brought the two of us to this surreal time and place. No matter. I was here for him now; the past be damned. By the time we returned to the house, the coming night didn't seem so formidable. We would get through it—together.

*　*　*

I rose at 5:30 the next morning to prepare for Baby B's first clinic appointment. We made our way through the obstacle course to Shriners, and I signed in at the Burn Clinic. Although the clinic didn't begin until 9:00, it was only 8:15 and the sheet was already filled with names. Oddly, a few adults sat in the waiting room but no children were present. The clerk retrieved the clipboard without looking up. "They'll call you in a little while."

The waiting room was furnished with interlocking plastic chairs, forming a wide U-shape across the room. Centered within the U-shape was a child's chair and table set and a stand-alone activity block. A foosball game table was on the other side of the room. A television hung suspended from the ceiling. Garish morning cartoons blitzed the screen. I selected a seat in the far corner near wide windows where sunlight streamed in and overlooked the courtyard and street below. Looking down, I saw people crisscrossing the medical buildings, each carrying their own baggage of thoughts.

The waiting room gradually filled with children, parents, and caretakers. I was glad that I had gotten there early enough to claim a spot away from the blasting cartoons and the throttling noise coming from adolescents playing the hockey table game. Baby B startled easily, and even I was beginning to suffer sensory overload from the competing noises.

While we waited to be called, I watched the children and adults. I had been fortunate to have healthy children—and health insurance. I never had to wait in a free clinic with an ill child or deal with an assortment of distant doctors. Was there something they knew that could help me navigate through this situation simply by being observant like a tourist in a foreign land? The bits of conversation I caught were peppered with both Spanish and English. Although I did not understand much of what was said, some things are universal.

For instance, it was apparent from the way they greeted each other that many of the women and children were reconnecting after long absences. "Ah, how she has grown!" or "His skin looks so good!" they exclaimed about one another's children. The younger children initially traded shy glances, but later despite their injuries, they were chattering and chasing one another. The adolescents, having grown accustomed to the realities of their altered bodies, moved about with confidence. Some had limbs amputated and others were wearing face shields, but no one stared, recoiled, or turned away. In this room, they were accepted, embraced, and encouraged. I thought about how different this environment must be for them compared to the outside world.

A young Hispanic boy sat down in the chair beside me. His face was shiny smooth on one side and bumpy and red on the other. An ear was missing, and little fluffs of hair sprouted from his scarred head. His hands were also bandaged. He peeked at the *Dora the Explorer* video playing on the portable DVD I brought to entertain Baby B. "You can watch," I said, turning it slightly toward the boy so that he had a better view. He gave me a shy smile, watched the video for a few minutes, then looked at Baby B.

"What his name?" he asked.

I told him Baby B's name and asked, "*¿Cómo se llama?*"

In a sweet, soft voice, lilting with accent, he told me his name was Miguel and that he and his mother were staying at the Ronald McDonald House. "My bandages off today," he added.

"That's great!" I responded.

"He have lot bandages," said Miguel, looking at Baby B.

Baby B's face, smooth and brown as an almond with huge brown eyes as bright as headlights, stood in sharp contrast to the white bandages wrapped around his head.

"*Si '*. They'll come off too, but not today."

"Okay, bye-bye," he said, walking, away as unexpectedly as he had appeared.

Parents and caretakers continued to arrive and leave with children. The white noise of multiple conversations filled the room.

Twice, women paused in front of Baby B. "*Que bonita la cara!*"

"*Gracias,*" I replied, thankful his face had been spared.

I had agreed that I would call Kanika as soon as they put us in the examination room. Three hours later she called me from across the street from John Sealy Hospital, where she was on duty.

"You still waiting?"

"Yup," I replied.

"I was hoping they'd at least have you in the examining room by now so I could run over and talk to his doctor."

"I overheard the clerks say he's not even here yet."

When Dr. H finally arrived, I called Kanika, and she rushed to Shriners. She was surprised to see us still sitting in the waiting room. "I thought you said Dr. H had arrived," she said.

"He has, but they still haven't called us yet."

"Hey, little man," she said, kneeling beside Baby B. He stared into her face, a small smile forming. "If they don't call you guys pretty soon, I'll go see what's the hold-up. I want to make sure he's seen before Dr. H goes back to surgery. If that happens, he won't get seen today at all."

"What do you mean? We've been here since 8 o'clock!"

"He performs surgeries at Sealy on the same day he sees kids here in the clinic."

"I don't get it," I said. "When we got here, lots of names were already on the sign-in sheet, but hardly anyone was in the waiting room. Now it's packed."

"I'm going to find out what's going on," she said. "This doesn't make sense."

I watched as she walked away, disappearing behind double doors.

Baby B flinched at the sudden noise as teenagers started jabbing away at the foosball game. On the opposite wall, the voices from a Spanish-language soap opera had replaced the morning cartoons.

I could tell from the agitated look on Kanika's face when she returned that she wasn't bringing good news.

"I tracked down the nurse coordinator," she said. "She recited some speech about waiting list rules. I told her when you signed Baby B in at eight, the sheet was full and hardly anyone was in the waiting room. She claimed she didn't know anything about that. I told her I'd be checking every fifteen minutes until he's seen."

In fifteen minutes, his name was called.

Months later we learned the truth about the Burn Clinic appointments—that it was run on a "first come, first serve" basis, not appointment time. Because many of the families were from out of the country, arrangements were made for them to be grouped at the same accommodations. Someone from the group went to Shriners, and as soon as the sign-in sheet was set out, he wrote in each child's name. Once we discovered that appointment times were irrelevant and patients were called based only on the sign-in sheet, we learned to play by clinic unwritten rules. One of us always went in early to put Baby B's name on the list. While it did not eliminate waiting hours for doctors to arrive at the clinic, it increased the likelihood that he would be seen on that day.

Once again, I found myself in the middle of a system that had its own code of operation. I didn't know it at the time, but that experience would be added to a long list of unwritten rules I would have to ferret out each time I sought services from any agency or organization whose mission was to help me help Baby B.

CHAPTER 21

Home for the Holiday

"Rest if you must, but don't you quit."

—*St. Augustine*

How ironic that Baby B's first birthday occurred the weekend of our evacuation from Galveston in the midst of stratospheric chaos and upheaval.

Within a few days after we returned to Galveston, Kanika sent birthday invitations to her friends and colleagues who knew about our history with Baby B. The next week my husband and Nicole drove in from Austin, and Alpha, who was by then Kanika's fiancé, flew in from Kansas City for the party. The room was filled with people from diverse backgrounds and professions, but we were all united in our wish for Baby B's well-being and continued healing.

The cake was decorated with Disney cartoons and palm trees. Nicole held Baby B in her arms and pointed to the single candle. Colorful streamers and balloons dangled from the ceiling. Lawrence circulated the room, snapping pictures. Sunshine filtered through the storm windows, cloudy with sea salt and age. Dust motes drifted through the room like stardust.

Everyone sang "Happy Birthday" in a low, slow melody. Otherwise, Baby B's hands would not fly up to cover his ears, quick as striking cymbals to ward off the sudden sound. He had never made the typical baby utterances during his time with us. Except for cries of distress or pain, he had continued to be mute. From Nicole's arms, he examined the crowd, wide-eyed and curious. I held my breath, trying to gauge his reaction. *Why can't I just enjoy the moment?*

"Happy Birthday, Baby B. You're one year old," said Kanika.

After she blew out the candle, we softly clapped. His hands shot up—but not to cover his ears. He pressed them together—one bandaged hand met the other—joining us in a silent clap.

Day to day, there had not been much to celebrate beyond our family's power to pull together, joining forces to do whatever it took to care for him. We did not know what the future held for him or, for that matter, ourselves. But that day we rejoiced in the fact that he was safely within our fold, holding court in a room filled with magic.

* * *

As the month passed, my mood mimicked the changing fall foliage. People imagine that island plant life is in a constant state of perennial happiness. Nothing is. The intense colors of tropical flowers disengaged and withered away against the continuous onslaught of August heat. Esperanza's sunny tubular face faded and the stems of spent annuals protruded from the earth like claws. The weathered bougainvillea branches shed their beautiful blossoms as the roots reached deep down to brace against the coming coastal winds and torrential rains.

As the October days grew shorter, the decreased light and lengthening shadows cast a dark cloud over Baby B. Daylight on the island retreated reluctantly like an angry child, palms waving wildly and the salty air electric with the sounds of waves crashing. On days when evening fog rolled in, structures and shrubs took on sinister shapes of things that might reach out and suck you in. By the time darkness fell, Baby B had worked himself into a fretting frenzy. I went from room to room, switching on lights to eliminate dark doorways and corners and put on soft background music to mute the murmurings of the old house settling in for the night. On the rare nights when he looked at me with recognition and connection and seemed comforted by my touch, I was grateful.

In late October, social services was still searching for other therapeutic foster care. Lawrence continued to arrive on Fridays from Austin, most of his time spent driving during the darkness because of daylight savings time. Lawrence, Kanika, and I managed to coexist amiably within the confines of the little bungalow on weekends. Although it was never voiced, we all understood that in such close quarters, there was little room for big drama.

The strain of being away from my home and husband and the feeling that strangers were in control of my daily life started to stretch me at the seams. My initial euphoria that I had been chosen to fulfill a mission of healing and love that no one else could execute slowly began to evaporate like the early morning mist rising off the bay. I envied Kanika's sixteen-hour day away and was no longer poised to greet Lawrence with open arms after his four-hour drive from Austin. All of my compassion and patience was poured into Baby B.

I had not asked anyone for help, but I secretly hoped that one day I would open the door to someone holding a casserole or offering to sit with Baby B and me through the difficult "sundowning" hours. I entered my "Woe is me" phase.

Finally, I called Craig, who managed our foster care placement. "I need to go home."

Silence.

"Is something wrong?" he asked.

"Yes. I've been here two months. My husband spends hours driving here every weekend. I need to go home."

"Okay . . . well, we do have respite. Is Kanika . . . ?"

"Kanika is at the hospital 24/7. What's respite?"

"We have caregivers who can step in temporarily, depending on how long you need. The hard part will be finding someone who can take care of Baby B's medical needs," he replied.

"Why can't I take him with me?"

"I don't understand; I thought you said you needed a break."

"I said I need to go home. I didn't say anything about leaving Baby B."

"Isn't he still getting daily physical therapy at Shriners? That's part of the therapeutic plan. That can't be stopped."

"I'm only talking about a weekend," I replied. "Leave on Friday, back on Sunday. He wouldn't miss any of his therapies. This wouldn't be the first time he's come to Austin with me. Except this time we wouldn't be on the roads for twenty-four hours running from a hurricane. As a matter of fact, I'd like to start taking him home every other weekend with me."

And so began the endless road expeditions Lawrence would make from Austin to Galveston, and Baby B and I would make from Galveston to Austin. On Fridays when I left Galveston, the departure had to be timed as efficiently as a jet taking off. If we were not crossing the causeway connecting the island to the mainland by noon, we were ensnared in peak hour traffic. Thursday nights I performed the preliminary packing, and on Friday mornings, immediately after Baby B's physical therapy, we made the four-hour drive. Compared to the hellish twenty-four-hour escape from Hurricane Rita, the commute was a cakewalk.

* * *

In early November, a social worker recently hired by Craig came to interview me despite the fact that Baby B was slated to be under the care of another foster family by the end of the month. Shirley was friendly and outgoing with a casual "just treat me like a part of the family" interview style. She arrived on Saturday morning as Kanika and I were finishing Baby B's bath. She sat in a chair across from the bed, where my daughter and I bent over Baby B, applying creams and ointments and wrapping his limbs. She watched us mimic each other's movements up and down his body like twin pianists at a single piano.

Afterward, Kanika carried Baby B to the kitchen for his breakfast. Shirley remained in the room, asking me a series of questions about my background and family history while I recapped jars and gathered towels and sheets. Although it was her job, I felt uncomfortable revealing my personal life to a stranger scribbling away on a yellow legal pad and thought that her time could have been better spent finding a permanent family for Baby B.

When Shirley finally left two hours later, I closed the door and took a deep breath. Later, however, I thought of questions I should have asked. *Given the twenty-four-hour vigil and specialized care Baby B required, would a visiting nurse be possible? How close was the agency to finding another family?*

It was almost Thanksgiving. My promise to Lawrence that I would be back home by then seemed highly unlikely. On Monday I called Craig and reminded him of our agreement. "You said by Thanksgiving you would have someone else. We're two weeks away."

"Finding another family that meets all of Baby B's needs is proving more difficult than we anticipated," he said. "We've contacted several and some expressed interest initially, but when they hear about the daily trips to Shriners for therapy and the clinic and the amount of home care required, they don't think they can handle it."

"Well, it's better they tell you that up front, so they're not calling you up in a week saying they can't do it anymore. But I have to be home for Thanksgiving, Craig. I need to see my grandkids and besides, I promised my husband from the very beginning that I'd be home by Thanksgiving—for good."

"Maybe . . . I can get an emergency placement for him, but it will only be temporary. As a last resort, I'll have to start looking at some type of facility."

"What kind of facility?" I asked.

"Somewhere there's personnel to meet his medical needs and transport him back and forth to Shriners," he answered.

"Facility? You mean some kind of nursing place?"

"I'm running out of options," he replied.

My mind raced. Being in the care of a constantly changing cadre of caregivers would destroy him. "I can take him home with me over Thanksgiving," I heard myself say. "Shriners isn't scheduling therapy again until after the holidays anyway. We'll talk about where you are in a permanent placement when I come back."

Craig agreed without hesitation. I was sure he was relieved to be free of the grueling task of finding a replacement for me during Thanksgiving. After hanging up, I rewound the conversation in my head. *What had I just agreed to?*

*   *   *

Of all the major holidays, Thanksgiving, falling on my birthday was the most stressful. My parents treated the day of my birth like the leftover turkey, wrapping it up quickly and putting it away. In the toxic environment of my childhood home, any holiday was fraught with increased tension, misunderstanding, and often violence. However, it was at the intersection of my birthday and Thanksgiving feast that I felt the full force of an empty childhood.

Having my own family enabled me to let go of childhood disappointments and begin creating happy traditions for my children. However, it took years before I was able to relax and truly enjoy the holidays without feeling personally responsible for orchestrating everyone's happiness. I wasted an enormous amount of energy scurrying around and worrying that something I said or did might make someone unhappy. It was as if I were still stuck in that little girl mode, waiting for something to go wrong, the scary pumpkin to explode. Ghosts from my childhood floated into my adult psyche and undermined the happiness I should have felt surrounded by my loving, boisterous bunch. I was about to add to my mix of holiday angst and insecurities by bringing home a baby that needed constant attention.

I knew that Lawrence wanted the best for Baby B and had done everything within his power to make it possible for me to stay in Galveston, but I expected his patience to dissipate at some point.

"I've got good news and bad news," I said when he answered the phone. "Which do you want first?"

"Good news."

"I'll be home for Thanksgiving. We can have a big family dinner with the kids."

"That's great! We'll probably need both cars to bring all your stuff back. I'll take a day off from work to come help you pack. Now, what's the bad?" he asked.

"I have to come back after Thanksgiving." I rushed forward to fill in the awkward silence that followed. "Just until December. By then they'll have a family ready for Baby B." I pretended this was fact rather than just another vague promise proffered by Craig.

"Where is he going to be until then?"

"Oh, didn't I tell you? He's coming home with me. He'll stay with us through Thanksgiving weekend and then we'll go back to Galveston with Kanika for a little while longer, and that will be it." I belted it out all in one breath and waited for the backlash. But once again I underestimated my husband's generous spirit.

"Anything you want me to do to help get the house ready for Thanksgiving?" he asked.

"How about vacuuming?" I said teasingly.

"Okay."

"Seriously?"

"Sure."

"The whole house? It's hard work you know, not as easy as cutting the yard," I said, laughing.

"I think I can handle it," he said, laughing with me.

The next day, I called Nicole and asked her if she could do the Thanksgiving grocery shopping.

"Just tell me what to get," she said. "It can't be that hard."

I smiled at her remark. It was the first time in my married life I would not be home shopping, cleaning, and cooking for a holiday.

*   *   *

I arranged to leave Galveston immediately after Baby B's Tuesday physical therapy appointment. If everything ran according to my carefully planned schedule, we would miss rush hour traffic and arrive in Austin well before dark.

Shirley called Monday evening. "Baby B's relatives will be in Galveston on Tuesday. They want to see him."

"What?" I asked. "I've already talked to Craig. I'm leaving for Galveston Tuesday morning with Baby B."

"You'll have to wait until after they've seen him. There's nothing we can do."

I hung up the phone and fumed all day until Kanika came home. "This is so unfair!" I said to her that evening. "They couldn't come 'see' him while he was in the hospital—when he really needed them—but they can just show up, and we have to put everything on hold so they can have a little holiday visit?"

"I know, Mom. You're right, but there's nothing we can do about it."

Where had I heard that before? I wanted her to join me in my rant.

"Well, how is this supposed to work?" I asked, my voice rising. "They sure can't come to this house." I was caught up in a whirlpool of emotions. I was not going to have the sanctuary we had created for Baby B invaded, and yet I could not bear the thought that I was expected to bundle him up and deliver him to them. As if she could read my thoughts, Kanika put her arm around my shoulder.

"Don't worry, Mom. I'll call Shirley and make arrangements to take him to her office. I'll come home from the hospital and pick him up. Shirley can call me when the visit is over, and I'll pick him up and bring him back to you."

Would he even recognize them? When he awoke in that stark hospital among strangers in an altered body reeling with pain, where were they then? Not one came during his entire hospitalization. Not one came when he was discharged from Shriners. Did they have a change of heart? Was there something Shirley was not telling us? Would I ever see him again?

Tuesday afternoon, I sat on the couch, cradling Baby B closely, the packed diaper bag at my feet. Kanika walked through the door, and we exchanged glances. "Ready for me to take him?" she asked.

I was like a child clinging to her most prized possession. I handed him over.

"I'll bring him back in a little while, Mom."

I closed the door quickly to shut out the brightness. I paced in and out of the rooms, searching for something. I could have walked to the beach or around the block, but crashing waves of conflicting emotions trapped me inside. *Shouldn't I feel relief that his family is finally showing up? Was it possible they only recently discovered his whereabouts? News accounts carry stories every day about fractured families losing track of one another. Now that they know, they will do the right thing.*

When I finally meet them, I will share Baby B's journey through terrible pain and isolating hospitalization. I will tell them how much my family and I have grown to love him, holding tight in the eye of the storm. "No, no need to thank us," I will say. "We feel honored and blessed to have opened our lives and our hearts to this beautiful baby."

Letting go will not be easy, of course. But I would find comfort in the fact that he would go to those who truly loved him, not to a bureaucracy of foster homes and institutions.

I went over the various scenarios in my mind, fine-tuning, clipping, and snipping at them like a filmmaker striving to arrive at the perfect ending until I was jolted back by the ring of the telephone.

"We're on our way back," said Kanika.

"Already?"

"I'll tell you about it when I get there."

"Well, that didn't take long," I said as Kanika walked through the door with Baby B. I reached for him. His limbs stiffened and splayed out, startled by our movements.

"It's okay, it's okay," I whispered, taking him.

"Yeah, I thought it would take at least an hour," she said.

"Did you see them?" I asked.

"No. Shirley met me outside and she took Baby B. I couldn't have been gone more than twenty minutes when she called just as I was pulling into the hospital parking lot and said I should come pick him up. By the time I got back, the family had left. Shirley said each time one of them tried to hold him, he started screaming and basically never stopped. She said the family was surprised by his appearance . . . the bandages and everything. Couldn't wait to get out of there."

"What did they expect?" I said. "Too bad they didn't see him at the hospital three months ago when he really needed them, when he was going to the tub room every day. Maybe they wouldn't be so *surprised*. Maybe they'd be used to it by now."

I looked down at him, exhausted and asleep in my arms. I pictured him in a crammed, airless office surrounded by a blur of strange faces, passed along lap to lap, held in the loose arms of those whose hearts had already let him slide away.

"Before they left, Shirley said she asked them if they wanted to talk about plans for Baby B now that he was out of the hospital. They said, 'No.' They were just visiting someone during the holiday and stopped by to see how he was doing."

"What?" I asked, not for clarification but out of disgust.

"Yeah. This was just a little side trip on their way to somewhere better, I guess."

"They say anything about the mother?" I asked.

"No, I don't think she was even mentioned."

"Well, at least we're free to take him home with us for Thanksgiving. At least they didn't drag it out pretending they cared," I said.

I watched Kanika slowly pull objects from the pockets of her white coat like a magician extracting scarves from a bag of tricks: notepad, penlight, stethoscope, and finally cell phone. She peered at the screen. "I've got to get back to the hospital," she said. "What time do you want to leave tomorrow?"

"As soon as we can," I replied. "Going through Houston the day before Thanksgiving is going to be terrible if we don't make it out of here before noon."

Baby B's sundowning episodes had been gradually decreasing in their intensity, but that evening they resurfaced full force. As the light outside faded and the muted tones of the last hours of the day spread through the house, Baby B went into alert mode. His little body leaned forward and his head tilted slightly, listening. Street noises streamed in: ambulance sirens, motorcycle pistons, dogs barking, people shouting. In his heightened state, perhaps he could even hear the palm fronds flapping. Inside, the rotating sounds of the washing machine and dishwasher or the sudden swish of the heating system kicking on were enough to make him whimper.

By bedtime, he was into full meltdown. It was past midnight before the ghosts of the past turned him loose.

Do not despair, dear Baby B. They will not return to claim you.

*   *   *

I looked forward to going home, but my son and his family would also be arriving the same night, and the next day would be Thanksgiving. I felt overwhelmed. I called my husband and daughter to tell them that Kanika, Baby B, and I would be home the following day. Lawrence joked about vacuuming the house being as grueling as pushing a lawnmower, and Nicole said that after grocery shopping for Thanksgiving, she could really appreciate all the years I had done it. Their words were like a salve to my soul.

Kanika and I shared the driving and by 2 p.m., Wednesday, we arrived back home in Austin ready to savor the next few days with family. My husband and Nicole proudly displayed their housekeeping and grocery shopping skills and shared caring for Baby B while Kanika and I relaxed.

Later that night my son, daughter-in-law, and three grandchildren arrived. All day I had anticipated their arrival, but the sounds of the doorbell ringing, the door opening, and the flood of voices rushing in overtook me with an unexpected wave of emotion. It had only been a few months since I'd seen them, but it seemed like much longer. I heard one of the children say, "Where's Nana?"

"She's in the bedroom," my husband replied.

Pounding feet raced up the stairs, a stampeding herd. I sat against the headboard, looking toward the doorway, Baby B lying contently next to me. Three small figures appeared simultaneously at the entrance, standing so close they looked glued together.

"Hey there," I said. "Come on over and meet Baby B."

They advanced cautiously, moving in unison. I hoped their parents had prepared them sufficiently so that they would not be shocked by Baby B's bandages. I was glad that his head was no longer wrapped in bandages and hoped the beauty of his enormous brown eyes and smooth, sweet face would draw them in.

Side by side, they inched over to the bed.

Rashaad, age five, asked, "Why is he muddy?" He stared at the parts of Baby B's arms and hands that were uncovered and were dark and ripply from burns.

"His skin is hurt, but it will be better soon."

Myah, three, stared silently.

"Are you going to keep him?" asked eleven-year-old Malik. He asked it as casually as sipping a cool drink.

The question hit me full force—like ice water to the face— and took my breath away. I stammered out some reply cloaked in adult avoidance code that children instantly recognize.

"We're taking care of him until he's better."

"When will that be?"

"Don't know yet."

* * *

The next morning I made sure my grandchildren were downstairs before I gave Baby B his bath treatments. I did not want them to see or hear the raw reality of his injuries. Afterward, he watched the rambunctious and boisterous behavior of my grandchildren the same way he stared at the colorful mobile dangling from his crib. The only children he had been in the company of were at Shriners, and many of those were as silenced as he from the shock of their injuries.

For months he and I were as bound together in our Galveston cocoon as the bandages that confined him. I had worried about the impact of his being suddenly cast into the midst of the activity of a large household with unfamiliar faces and voices. However, observing happy, active children seemed to offer a positive distraction for him—and for me also. Surprisingly, I did not feel driven to monitor each person's happiness meter.

Sometime during the night I woke to Baby B's screams. By the time I stumbled into my office where we had set up a portable crib, my son already had Baby B in his arms, pacing back and forth and whispering comforting words: *"You're all right. You're all right."*

"Want me to take him?" I asked.

"No, we're okay."

I took a seat at my desk. Amber light streamed out from a crack in the closet door onto the papers and pens that lay in the same spot I left them three months ago. What was the last thing I did in quiet meditation here? Compose a poem? Write a short story? Now I sat in muted darkness maintaining a vigil with my son as he treaded the floor soothing a stranger's son. I felt as though I were in a cinema watching a scene unfold before me. It was the most intimate setting I had shared with my son in years. It felt strange and wonderful.

"You're pretty good at that," I offered.

"Kimberly and I have been getting up in the middle of the night walking babies for a long time," he replied.

After a while, Baby B went back to sleep in my son's arms, and he lowered him gently into the crib. I switched off the light, and my son and I said a soft "Good night."

CHAPTER 22

Eye of the Heart

"You don't make room for a baby in your home. You make room in your heart."

—Anonymous

FEW WEEKS AGO I had been in Galveston cerebrating Baby B's birthday. A few days ago, I had been distressed over the sudden arrival of his absentee relatives. But I kept my promise to my husband that I would be home on Thanksgiving Day. In addition, my daughters and my son and his family were there to celebrate my birthday. In the midst of the festivities was Baby B, the stranger at the table—except there was nothing strange about him being among us. It seemed as natural as the scent of turkey and dressing and sweet potato pie. And although my son, his wife, and his children were strangers to him, Baby B never once shrieked in fear when they held him. He accepted them as fully as they accepted him.

As I sat in physical therapy holding Baby B the following week, I remembered fondly our family sitting on the stairwell landing in Austin, surrounding him like a protective herd.

"Hold him firmly on your lap," said Claire as she approached with what looked like a miniature chainsaw.

She lowered the spinning blade to the cast. I suppressed the urge to say, "Be careful," as the jagged whirling wheel made contact with it. Amazingly, Baby B did not flinch or draw back. He listened to the whirring noise and watched the blade with fascination, while I watched with fear. She cut open the cast, then cleaned and examined his hand and molded another cast.

As we prepared to leave, she said, "In a few weeks, once we've completed casting, we'll need to fit him for a burn suit."

"What's a burn suit?" I asked, imagining some sort of shimmering silver space garment.

"I'll show you."

I followed her into the hall in front of a cabinet with rows of pullout drawers. Garments of various colors were inside the drawers. She pulled out a long-sleeved blue T-shirt and matching bottom. The set, a smooth stretchy material, looked like doll clothes.

"How's he supposed to fit into that?" I asked.

"It'll stretch to fit his body. It works to compress and smooth the scars."

"How long will he have to wear it?"

"A year or more," she replied. "It depends on how rapidly his skin heals."

"Even in the summer . . . the heat?"

"We send kids back to Mexico who live in little adobes out in the desert; they do just fine," she said. Then she added, "And they don't even have air conditioning."

How do you know "they do just fine"?

*　*　*

On Thursday morning I exited the elevator for Burn Clinic with Baby B, trying not to inhale the familiar acrid chemical odor. I turned the corner and winced at the sight of the packed waiting room. I clung to the hope that a true schedule would eventually evolve even though everything pointed against that prospect. Nevertheless, I packed enough snacks, toys, DVDs, and diapers to get us through hours in the waiting room. I learned to expect the unexpected. One time a beauty queen arrived with her entourage. I watched as children surrounded her and looked up at her perfect face and the tiara that sat atop her perfect hair. Another time, I saw leather-clad muscular members of Bikers for Abused Children deliver armloads of gifts. Then there was the time three women dressed in flowing abayas floated silently into the room and sat stoically against a wall. Even with all the pressures and stresses concentrated into that small area, I never witnessed any negative outburst or loss of control among the adults or the children.

Eventually we were called to the exam room, where we waited another hour for the medical rounds team to reach us. Baby B was thirteen months old, but his legs were still too weak from the burns and surgeries to support him. I passed the time in the narrow hallway outside the room, holding him under the arms in a simulated walking activity (stepping signals to the brain) while I watched the cluster of white coats stream in and out of rooms like spilled cream. When the rounding team was a few doors from our room, I called Kanika, and she rushed over from John Sealy Hospital. The doctors spent less than twenty minutes in each room. I knew that we would have only a brief window of time to glean information and ask questions. I was depending on her, trained in their language, to beat the ticking clock.

Two residents, four medical students, two physical therapists, nutritionist, nurse, physician assistant, social worker, and Dr. K, the surgeon, crowded into the room. They stood silently before the examining table, all eyes trained on Baby B, stripped bare except for his diaper. Kanika and I stood to each side of him, two centurions.

Looking out into the sea of faces, I recognized only a few. I knew enough about how things were done by now to know that most of them were only getting a brief overview of Baby B's current medical condition and prognosis and hadn't a clue about the history behind his injuries. Someone said "scalded." *I hope they don't think I did this terrible thing.* I immediately felt ashamed that I cared what any of them thought.

The feeling that I was being judged whenever I was in public with Baby B—standing in a checkout line or sitting under a shaded tree with him at the playground—was a feeling like rising nausea I had to learn to suppress. Because it was obvious his were not injuries caused by a birth defect. No. These were injuries caused by someone's neglect or abuse—and the accusing eyes rested on me. Of course, part of this scenario was created in my mind because I knew Baby B's history, but the stares were not imaginary.

On the island, in addition to Shriners, there was a burn unit at John Sealy Hospital, so townspeople were used to coming into contact with burn victims. Also as a rule, it was a community that seemed to accept people's differences without comment. But I was determined that both Baby B and I learn to live comfortably and bravely outside of that environment.

Dr. K stepped forward and gently placed Baby B's right hand in his palm. He shook his head slowly. "This is an abuse case." He asked the therapist about the hand therapy, concluding that he was concerned about the hand's appearance.

Claire interjected, "As bad as it is doctor, it's much better than it was." The doctor peppered the others on the team with questions regarding ongoing therapies. Kanika voiced specific concerns about the healing process.

Dr. K was one of several surgeons who would perform the

numerous surgeries Baby B would undergo at Shriners. Now that his life had been saved, all future efforts were directed toward preventing infections and rebuilding his body. "Let's schedule the next surgery for January," he said. There was always a next surgery. The white coats retreated, sliding out of the room like white foam at low tide.

"What do you think, Mom? Have any questions?" Kanika asked.

"Not right now. Maybe later."

"Okay. I gotta get back." She gave me a quick hug. "We'll talk tonight."

Claire remained in the room to give me extra instruction on bandaging. She lamented the lack of appreciation surgeons had for the work and dedication that physical therapists put into rehabilitating children. "They think we should be able to work miracles—give kids back what God gave them. But we can never do that."

* * *

December slipped in with shorter and colder days. The heavy drapery of clouds blocked out the tropical sun and blue sky. Nights were saturated in a gray fog that surrounded the island like a shroud. Billboards and buildings receded behind an opaque curtain of murky mist.

The daily drudgery of clinic appointments, toilsome therapies, and terrible nights gradually led to numbness that mimicked normalcy. I avoided looking in the bathroom mirror because the dispirited face that stared back at me seemed so disconnected from the person I once was. I had reached the final stage of grief: acceptance.

It was during this time of mental inertia that the news I no longer anticipated arrived. It came on one of Kanika's rare evenings home from the hospital. We were nestled in a layer of blankets on the couch with Baby B between us, the three of us encapsulated in the television's blue light. The white noise of whatever we were watching acted as a welcome buffer against thinking or talking. We had finished Baby B's bath and bandage routine and were savoring the satisfaction of one finished task before beginning the next.

"Social services called today," Kanka said.

"What now?" I asked, not really wanting to know. I expected her to say they wanted more paperwork. There was always a report to submit, some form to fill out. Papers accumulated in piles on tables and counters like clumps of seaweed on the beach.

"They've found a place for Baby B."

I froze. "Who? Where?"

"He's a retired burn doctor. He's fostering two elementary school-age kids with burns now."

"A burn doctor. That's good," I said. "He knows what to do."

"Yes. He makes sure they are in good shape before they leave."

"What do you mean, 'Before they leave'?" I asked.

"They send kids to him until they've recovered enough from the injuries to go to a foster home or a children's home."

"That's terrible."

"I know."

I looked down at Baby B. He had drifted off to sleep, his face set in serene blissful slumber. He still woke screaming. But not every night. I wondered where he would be sleeping in the future. How many different beds?

*   *   *

Five months ago I had strolled naively into a medical facility I didn't know existed. Until Kanika became an intern at the hospital, I, like the thousands of other tourists who vacationed on the island, never knew a Shriners Hospital was just a few blocks away. It is rarely, if ever, mentioned in Galveston brochures or magazines or the media at large. The fact that the island failed to promote a premier facility dedicated exclusively to saving children's lives and helping restore their bodies was a mystery to me.

On the other hand, island residents accepted the children as part of the community. They did not gawk or look uncomfortably away as if they had come upon something shameful. One restaurant on the island welcomed Shriners patients to eat for free.

One of my first forays into the larger community was to a Target store. Baby B sat on a thick blanket to cushion his tender bottom in the shopping cart. At the checkout, the clerk glanced at his burn suit and bandaged hands and asked if he was a "Shriners baby."

"Yes," I answered, buffering myself for the next question or comment: "How did it happen? Poor thing!" But those weren't her words.

"They work miracles there," she said smiling. "He's a cutie."

Occasionally, children could be seen silhouetted against the evening sky when the sun was subdued, walking stiffly or being pushed along the seawall in a wheelchair. Rather than bright swimsuits, they wore burn suits. Caps covered sensitive scalps and shaded fragile faces, shielding against the rays sun worshippers so passionately sought.

I was part of their world now. I sat next to those children in clinics. I saw the fear and confusion in their eyes as they were forced to adjust to a new reality, and a new body. Unlike the rest of the world, I knew they existed.

* * *

The next day Kanika came home for a short break before returning to the hospital for night duty.

"We need to talk," I said.

She plopped down beside me. "What's up?"

"I've been thinking about Baby B and this burn doctor."

"Um-ummm," she replied.

"I think it would be cruel to let him go now. He recognizes us; he's comfortable with us; he trusts us. It sounds like a good thing that there's this retired burn doctor they've found, but we don't know anything about him. He's taking care of two other children with burns. How much time is that going to leave for Baby B? Besides, nobody is going to take better care of him than we do—or care more."

"I agree," she said. "What do you want to do?"

What do *I* want? I hadn't been asked that question in a long time. "Well, I can't even imagine raising another child at this stage of my life," I began. "Your dad and I were just starting to do all the things we've been putting off for all these years before Baby B came into our lives. I've been thinking . . . there is one person in our family who would be perfect for Baby B." Kanika looked into my eyes searching, and then we both whispered simultaneously, "Nicole."

We knew how much Nicole loved children. She could not pass a baby without genuflecting. She loved working with children as a teacher. More importantly, she already knew Baby B. She was single with no children, which meant she would have the time and energy to devote to him. Most of all, she possessed the quality he needed more than anything else: a compassionate, caring heart. It seemed the perfect solution. And she would never need to shoulder the responsibility alone. Our family would always be the foundation, the support, the village.

But as with most things we had to slash through in our zest to rescue Baby B, the road to the destination was never, ever smooth. As quickly as we dismantled one blockade, someone assembled another.

CHAPTER 23

Where There's a Will

"If trying to find a way when you don't even know you can get there isn't a miracle; then I don't know what is."
—*Rachel Joyce*

WHEN HE CALLED that night, I didn't tell my husband about the retired burn doctor or about my conversation with Kanika regarding Nicole and Baby B. Ours was an insular family, and what I was contemplating seemed out of context with its core composition. My husband's mother and extended family lived in another state. I was estranged from my mother and siblings. After my father died, my mother retreated from her children, and we siblings retreated from one another. It had been years since any of us had any contact. I wondered if that was the legacy of growing up in an abusive household.

I knew that I was about to suggest something to Lawrence that would change the trajectory of our family forever. Only later did I realize there would be no trajectory—no clear path to where we were going. I did not know anything about the future except that Baby B's future depended on our decision.

When Lawrence called the following evening, I told him about the social services plan to stabilize Baby B with the burn doctor and then to destabilize him by moving him from place to place.

There was a moment of silence before he said, "Maybe they'll find someone once he's better."

"Miracles do happen, but kids with special needs, disabled, disfigured . . . they probably won't. Kanika and I were thinking maybe . . ."

"Yeah, what?"

"About asking Nicole what she thinks about adopting him. You know she said that she wants to be a foster mother one day. She loves children. She's great with him. What do you think?"

"I think that's a great idea" he said. "Ask her. She'd make a great little mother."

Nicole was a petite woman, on the shy side of five feet. After Lawrence and I said good night, I thought about how outgoing and bubbly she was. Baby B would become the recipient of her huge heart, and he would continue to be a part of ours—a win/win proposition.

I called Nicole the following night. She did not need convincing. I had barely finished sharing my thoughts with her when she broke in: "Mama, you know I've always said I was going to be a foster mother someday and adopt. Looks like someday is here!"

"Are you sure you don't want to think about it? I don't need an answer right away. Nothing is going to change anytime soon. Right now I'm just letting Craig know that I'm willing to keep taking care of Baby B as his foster mother without a time limitation. I haven't said anything to him about the possibility of your adopting him."

"No. I don't need to think about it. It's not like I haven't helped take care of him already. He knows me. He's a sweet baby."

*   *   *

Craig received the news with happy restraint. He said he would start the paperwork. The following week I met him at Shriners to sign a contract declaring that I was the "permanent foster mother." My hand paused above the signature line seeing the word "permanent." What did that really mean? I signed the document.

Nothing changed on the surface. I took Baby B to therapy at Shriners daily and outpatient clinic twice a month. Kanika continued to come home after marathon time at the hospital and walk the extra mile with Baby B and me through the night. But below the surface, an emotional shift occurred. I was now legally empowered to act on Baby B's behalf.

I wondered what effect, if any, my official title would have in my day-to-day interactions at the hospital. Even though I was held responsible for his well-being, I felt outside the sphere of influence when decisions were made regarding his care. Once at the clinic, a nurse taking intake information glanced up at me and said, "So you're just the caretaker, right?"

Stung and insulted, I replied, "Yes that's all I am."

To his credit, he immediately realized the insensitivity of his remark and apologized. He was the latest replacement in a series of nurses managing the outpatient clinic. "I'm going to straighten things out in this department," he boasted at one point. "In six months, you won't recognize it." But in six months he too was also gone, having succumbed to the same hospital politics and disorganization.

Although I was a permanent fixture in Baby B's life, I felt I was viewed as a temporary installation, here today and gone tomorrow. Perhaps I was partially responsible because I was reluctant to speak out, choosing to remain silent when I disagreed with or silently questioned some aspect of treatment. Until one morning when I literally turned a corner. Baby B had to stay in the hospital overnight for tests and an early-morning procedure. I had left the hospital late the night before after he was medicated and sleeping, returning early the next morning to find his room flooded in fulgent fluorescence. He was alone, his eyes wide and staring out as if he were in shock. His bandages were unraveled, his arms exposed and bloody from scratching.

I ran to the nurse's station where two nurses stood next to a long, curved counter, conversing. "You need to come to Baby B's room. He's all bloody!" I shouted. "He's bleeding!" One ran back to the room with me and immediately started wiping away the blood with antiseptic and applying clean wrappings. She gave him meds to quell his itching and anxiety.

I felt sick to my stomach. Kanika and I had worked hard to heal his wounds so that new skin could begin forming, maintaining an around-the-clock vigil in an effort to prevent this very thing. When skin is regenerating, the intense urge to scratch is maddening. Imagine if it is occurring simultaneously on over sixty-five percent of your body. If there were a way to gouge his way through the layers of bandages and wrappings, he found it. Once nails and flesh contact, the threat of infection spirals upward. Right there, hovering over him as the nurse tended to him, I made a vow that he would never again be left alone in any hospital—not for a second.

I had a passing acquaintance with Zalena, the nurse who had returned with me to Baby B's room. She was a diminutive woman with soft brown eyes and dark curly hair that framed her face like a lion's mane. She had a quiet confidence and supported families with enthusiasm and encouragement. It meant a lot to have someone with a ready smile in such sad surroundings. After Baby B had been medicated, bandaged, and made as comfortable as possible, she asked me to step into the hall, guiding me to a secluded corner.

"He's yours now," she said. "You're the one who has primary responsibility for him. You have to be more visible and vocal about your expectations for his care. I'm just coming on for the morning shift, but they have been trying to get a doctor to come write orders for the anxiety and itching. You have to let them know he has somebody that is watching out for him now."

I was not sure who "them" was. The doctors? The nurses? Shriners? Social services? Where to start? Before Baby B, I had the good fortune of having minimum experience with hospitals and zero with social service agencies. As a consequence, my timidity and reticence to confront problems was proving to be detrimental to Baby B. Zalena's call to arms struck a chord. I wish she could know how her words would reverberate repeatedly in the years to come, girding me up to stand on his behalf and bolstering me for the battles ahead.

*   *   *

Kanika did not have time off for Christmas to leave Galveston, so Lawrence and Nicole joined us there. On Christmas mornings, no matter how warm and sunny Texas was, the fantasy of snowflakes drifted through my mind. On Galveston Island, the gray morning fog rolling in from the Gulf was as close to a white Christmas as we were going to get.

A little artificial tree with tiny twinkling lights sat in the corner, almost hidden behind the mountain of gifts for Baby B. Lawrence and I sipped coffee while we watched Kanika and Nicole alternately open gifts and cradle Baby B. He wore a red Santa Claus bib and cap. It had been years since Lawrence and I had experienced the magic a child radiates on Christmas morning. Baby B had that same wide-eyed expression my children had so long ago. The joy of being together that morning vanquished the horrors of the past months. Now that he was legally entrusted to our family, I felt an emotional guardrail disappear. I could love and accept him without fear of what the next day might bring.

The following week I drove back home to Austin with Baby B to bring in the New Year with my husband. My son and his wife dropped off our three grandchildren for the night and left with his sisters to ring in 2006. Again Baby B delighted in watching my three grandchildren's antics and ongoing activity. His eyes widened and his mouth formed an "O" slowly, spreading to a smile. I think it fascinated him to watch children not bound by physical restraints and limitations. He fell asleep watching them.

Lawrence and I stayed awake watching videos with the kids and eating snacks until horn blasts and noisemakers alerted us that the next year had arrived. I had made New Year's resolutions in the past to lose a few pounds or to start or finish a project, but not this time. I had given up the false expectation that I could predict my future. I simply resolved to stay connected to those whom I loved.

CHAPTER 24

A System Out of Touch

"Hope is like a bird that senses dawn and carefully starts to sing while it is still dark."
                                          —Martin Luther King, Jr.

F INALLY IN FEBRUARY 2006, one year, four months, and two weeks after I first walked into Baby B's hospital room, Kanika told me that Dr. S pronounced that Baby B had progressed enough to continue physical therapy in Austin as long as he returned to Shriners outpatient clinic once a month. As with the other surgeons who rotated in and out of treating Baby B, I had never met Dr. S. Kanika pointed him out as he hurried down the hospital hall.

"There's the doctor who admitted Baby B," she said.

He was also Baby B's surgeon through the most critical phase of hospitalization. Dr. S was of average height with a slender frame, sandy hair, and wire-rimmed glasses, and he was an expert in the field of child burns. He moved with a swiftness and steadiness that propelled him forward, past distractions.

His manner did not invite access. Even though he had taken your child's life into his hands, his availability to you was transitory, at best. Maybe he believed that the nature and intensity of his specialty required that the primary focus of his time and energies be devoted to the child. Treatment and recovery were constantly shifting positions of ups and downs. Perhaps keeping a professional distance was his way of riding that roller coaster.

The discharge instructions consisted of a daily ritual for preventing the risk of life-threatening microbes: examine every inch of his body for signs of infection, bathe him in antibacterial solutions, apply antibacterial ointment. The threat of a consuming skin infection made post-burn treatment a rocky ride. In the charged environment of superbugs, I was saddled with the responsibility of taking super precautions to prevent their invasion of Baby B's vulnerable body. As long as infection was absent, we could return to Austin.

His tiny burn suit would continue to serve as an additional layer of protection against infection and in reducing scarring as his skin healed. Ongoing physical therapy would be essential to keeping his limbs flexible. Check, check, and check. I had been doing these things for more than a year. Nothing would change, except I would be home.

One more thing: He needed a Medicaid card, insurance to which all foster children are entitled. As long as Baby B remained on the island, an oasis of medical care would surround him, but as soon as he left, he would be stranded in the desert.

I shared that important concern with Claire, expecting sympathy. Instead, she said, "There's no hurry. There's nobody out there that knows how to provide therapy for burn kids like Shriners. I love Baby B. As far as I'm concerned, he could stay here until he's eighteen." I was both confused and infuriated by her statement. Was I that invisible in all this?

"Well, I can't stick around that long. I have a family waiting for me to come home."

She nodded her head in a way that indicated she had more to say, but decided against it.

The next day I spotted Andrea, the Shriners patient coordinator (alternately referred to as social worker) in the hospital hall and flagged her down. I assumed she had an office, but she had never invited me there to discuss long-term plans pending Baby B's discharge. All of our meetings were in the corridors, coincidental, and brief. She always had a stack of folders pressed against her chest like a shield, and checked her watch as a signal that she was ready to move on. She was the same person who had failed to find a foster family for Baby B when he was ready for discharge from the hospital. I asked her about getting Medicaid for Baby B so that he could receive physical therapy in Austin.

"Sure," she said. She pulled a notepad from the plethora of papers and folders she carried and wrote down an 800 number. "You call this number and they'll send you one." I gripped the paper tightly in my hand, the winning lottery ticket for my return to Austin.

"That's it?" I said, smiling up at her. "Just call this number?"

"Yep," she replied. "That's their number." She pointed her manicured nail at the paper and took off, heels clacking the floor like a toy hammer pounding pegs.

*   *   *

I exited the parking lot elated that I might be seeing the light at the end of the tunnel. I planned on calling the number after I gave Baby B his lunch and put him down for his nap. But the scrap of paper with the 800 number lying on the table and the thought that at the moment I could be talking to someone who could give me what I so desperately needed was too great. Holding the receiver between my face and shoulder, I fed Baby B applesauce and dialed. I heard a few ominous clicks, then a

busy signal. I hung up and called several more times with the
same result.

Understandable. Lunchtime. Lots of people calling.

Usually when Baby B took a nap, so did I. He still woke
up through the night, screaming and struggling against some
awful evil. I learned to sleep when he slept. That day instead of
sleeping, I held the phone in my hand and dialed again. Busy
signal. I called the operator.

"Yes, it's a legitimate busy signal."

I remember a friend telling me about winning a radio call-in
contest.

"Whenever I got a busy signal, I just kept hitting the redial
button," she said. "Eventually, I got through with the answer and
won the prize!"

I hit the redial button again and again but never hit the
jackpot. After two days I no longer needed the scrap of paper.
The number was as imprinted on my memory as my social
security number. I scattered calling throughout the day, waging
my own battle of will against machine. On the third day there
was a click and then a voice saying, "Hello."

I was so startled that I stuttered. "I'm calling about Medicaid."

"Yes, ma'am."

"I'm calling about a child I'm fostering."

"Fostering?"

"I'm the foster mother and he needs a Medicaid card."

"Name, social security number, date of birth."

Her voice was imperious. I held the receiver tighter to my
ear, alert for any hint I might be able to enlist effort from her on
my behalf.

"Mine or his?"

"His, ma'am."

"Okay, I have it right here," I replied.

Silence.

I assumed she had put me on hold after getting the information. As I waited, I jotted down appointments I would make for Baby B in Austin. A buzzing sounded in my ear. Disconnected.

The scenario was repeated in the coming weeks. Hours that should be devoted to giving Baby B my full attention or getting some rest were wasted. I was like the battered wife who returns again and again, hoping that things will be better the next time, only to be knocked down.

Each interaction was worse and more bizarre than the previous. Several times in the middle of my explaining why he needed a Medicaid card, the examiner simply said, "Sorry, ma'am, I don't know what you're talking about," and hung up. Each time I called I was forced to repeat the same words to a different person. I grew weary of hearing my own voice. The fact that Baby B came from another state with a complicated history seemed too big a leap for the interviewers. It was as if whoever was on the other end of the line had a checklist of questions and programmed answers and lacked the skills or the knowledge to deviate from the script.

I spotted Andrea one day at Shriners and ran to catch her before she disappeared around the corner.

"I'm having a hard time getting Baby B Medicaid." She looked at me as if I had just stated something as obvious as Monday follows Sunday.

"The people answering the calls have no idea what I'm talking about. Isn't that their job? There have been times they've actually hung up on me."

"You just have to keep working with them, get them to work with you. I tell our families they have to learn how to navigate the system for what they need because they're going to have to keep doing it once they leave Shriners." She glanced at her watch.

I resisted the temptation to ask, "If that is our job, what is yours?" But I did not want to alienate this woman who had the power to do more harm than good. It was apparent that she was primarily a paper-pusher. If I criticized her, she might push papers pertaining to Baby B to the bottom. I asked Shirley and Craig, my foster care contact, for help also, but their only reply was, "We can't get an answer either."

*   *   *

In the meantime, Lawrence and I continued to travel back and forth on alternating weekends. We performed drive-a-thons through traffic jams, car pile-ups, road detours, and bad weather. Anyone who has driven behind or beside an eighteen-wheeler in Texas on I-35 in a blinding rainstorm and/or hailstorm knows that while you are gripping the steering wheel, your heart is pounding like the pellets pelting the windshield. We didn't begrudge the cost of the commute in time, money, or inconvenience. It was worth being together, if only for forty-eight hours. Of course, there were irritations and arguments, but with limited time we resolved them quickly. Nicole came to help us with Baby B as often as she could. As usual, she added a lightness and laughter to trying times. I watched as she continued to bond with Baby B. The tenderness and warmth with which she handled him and his response by folding into her body was wonderful to watch.

Even though it is the shortest month, February in Galveston seemed endless. The dull, gray days stretched on endlessly. The sea was sleek and slow moving, barely touching the beach, which lay dormant as driftwood. The hollow shells of washed-up crabs lay strewn along the shoreline.

*   *   *

In March out of desperation I emailed the following letter to a public policy agency with the following subject line:

MEDICAID EMERGENCY

My name is Cynthia Bowen. I am an Austin resident, and permanent foster mother to an 18-month-old baby, a burn victim of neglect and abuse. I have had three social workers working with me for months trying to get Medicaid for the baby to no avail. The application has been misdirected, lost, found, and lingering in black hole, with no action taken. PLEASE HELP!

It was only one of many agencies that I contacted that never responded. At the supermarket one weekend, I spied a headline on the *Austin-American Statesman*:

Privately run benefits phone program for state criticized for waits, mix-ups

According to the article, Texas Health and Human Services officials were putting on hold a controversial call-in system staffed by low-wage, inexperienced private-sector customer service representatives. The system was plagued by long hold times and disconnects, and staffed by people who couldn't answer questions.

More than 127,000 children were dropped from health insurance programs. One policy analyst stated, "People aren't getting the services they need. They're not getting a lot of help, they're getting bounced around, their questions are not being answered at all or they're being given wrong information."

* * *

Finally. I had an answer. It was not because I wasn't persistent or lacked patience. It wasn't because I failed to explain myself adequately or Baby B's case was too complicated. It was because once again, the system had failed.

The same article contained a quote from Rep. Elliott Naishtat, D-Austin. "This is not acceptable." *Could he help me? Was it possible he might put action behind his words?*

On my return to Galveston, I called his office early Monday morning. I was transferred to Nancy Walker, his legislative director. She patiently listened to my ordeal, took all the necessary information, and promised to investigate and call me back as soon as she had an answer. She kept her word. A week later I received notification that Baby B's health coverage was approved. I was so relieved I cried.

Later I emailed Nancy to thank her profusely for taking such quick action and received this reply:

Glad we could be of help. It is unfortunate that it seems to take a phone call from a legislative office for a child to receive medical coverage. Sounds like Baby B is in good hands with you and that love will carry him through.

Rep. Naishtat has requested that the Commissioner of the Texas Health and Human Services Commission delay further implementation of the new call centers and integrated eligibility system until it has all the problems identified and resolved. We have not heard of any plan to delay as of yet or to address the system problems. You can be assured that our office will continue to work to ensure the system is working properly and that children and families are not falling through the cracks.

Please do not hesitate to contact us if you experience problems again.

Sincerely,
Nancy Walker, Legislative Director
Rep. Elliott Naishtat's Office

*   *   *

Kanika and I wheeled Baby B through Shriners' halls to pick up his final discharge papers and say good-bye to everyone who had been a part of the miracle of his recovery. On the burn unit, they recounted his days there and marveled at how far he had come. They commented on how his hair had grown back from having his head shaved on admission in order to harvest skin tissue for other parts of his body. They remembered his enormous brown eyes and long, ebony lashes. As we moved through the hospital, nurses and aides came out into the halls to wish us well. They pressed items into our hands: gauze, gloves, and bandages. I saw these items as symbolic gifts from the village we were leaving. It had taken this village to save this child.

Almost a year and a half after I had locked eyes with Baby B in that solitary hospital room, we were going home together.

PART III

Home

CHAPTER 25

Home

"I bear to witness the way love resurrects itself in the face of loss."

—*Kate Braestrup*

I REMEMBERED COMING HOME after the birth of each of my children happy, relieved, and slightly disoriented in addition to feeling a little apprehensive about my ability to do everything required for the new life for which I was responsible. Those feelings were present again as I settled into life with Baby B. However, unlike those first weeks home with my own children, hibernating and luxuriating in the routine of feedings, diaper changing, and naps, days with Baby B required constant vigilance and preparation. Although I was glad to be free of the stress of taking him to Shriners several times a week, I now spent the entire day, every day, alone with him. If I needed to go to the store, I had to wait for Lawrence to come home from work. Nicole worked and went to graduate school during the week, but on weekends I could always depend on her to help with Baby B and give Lawrence and me time off for a date night.

In May we returned to Galveston for a different reason—
to welcome another member to our family. Kanika Bowen
married Alpha Jallow, the man to whom she had been engaged
for the past year. During the times he had visited in Galveston,
he exhibited a strong, quiet confidence and was completely
supportive of her career. I thought he was the perfect partner
for her. As an act of respect, he called my husband and asked for
his blessing. With Alpha's job transfer to the Houston area, they
were ready to fully commit to one another.

My husband's mother and extended family travelled from
Oklahoma, and Alpha's relatives and friends flew in from
Gambia, London, and various part of the United States for the
ceremony. Nicole was the maid of honor. Our older grandson
Malik was a bridesmaid escort and younger grandson Rashaad
was ring bearer. Granddaughter Mayah was flower girl. Against
a background of palm trees, hibiscus, and esperanza—the
yellow flower of hope—Kanika and Alpha exchanged vows
promising to love, protect, and cherish one another.

*　*　*

Baby B was delayed in almost every aspect of his development.
How could he not be? He was unable to stand because of the
damage to his legs and feet or to hold objects because of the
damage to his hands. The hell that he survived had left him
confused and fearful. Despite all of these handicaps, when I
looked into his face I saw a keen intelligence. Trying to regain
stability must have been like swimming through murky water.
I pictured my family, encircling him like a school of dolphins,
guiding him through.

One of the first, and what turned out to be most important,
calls I made when I returned to Austin was to Early Childhood
Intervention (ECI). An occupational therapist from the child
life center at Shriners had given me the contact information

when she heard Baby B was returning to Austin with me. "Call them as soon as you get there. They can help you."

ECI is a federally funded intervention program for families with children birth to three, having disabilities and developmental delays. ECI therapists focus on working with children and families in their natural environment, whether that be the home, a relative's home, or childcare center. Research shows that growth and development are most rapid in the early years of life. The earlier problems are identified, the greater the chance of reducing their impact.

At the time, I had no idea what ECI was, but after two weeks home alone, I knew I needed help. Baby B's night terrors had never gone away, but after our return to Austin, they intensified with a vengeance. I was constantly in and out of his room throughout the night, checking his wrappings to make sure he had not dug through and damaged his skin. Sometimes as I looked into his crib, his eyes flashed open as if he were catching me in the act of something sinister. On good mornings, I looked into his sweet face and he smiled at me with clear-eyed recognition. On other mornings he screamed and recoiled at the sight of me. I remembered Psalm 23 as I staggered down the hall to his room:

> Even though I walk through the valley of the shadow of
> death,
> I will fear no evil, for you are with me;
> your rod and your staff, they comfort me.

During those first months in Austin, ECI therapists were my only adult contacts aside from my husband and Nicole. It was a completely alien experience for me to invite strangers into my home. The fact that they were there to observe my interaction with Baby B and to offer suggestions and advice on how that might be improved also took some getting used to. Fortunately, they were never critical and were always professional. They never intimated that they knew better than I what was best for Baby B—only that they could help me build upon my strengths. Consequently, I overcame my reticence and, more often than not, looked forward to their visits and advice.

On one particularly difficult morning, Judy, an ECI administrator, arrived for our appointment to find me near tears. Judy was scheduled to visit once a month to evaluate services Baby B received from ECI. I sat on the floor in our family room, Baby B on my lap. We clung loosely to one another like spent boxers. It was 11:30, but I had barely managed to brush my teeth, unfurl my hair, and throw on rumpled clothes. The curtains were open, but the summer light streaming in seemed like an affront.

Judy took a seat, and for a moment neither of us spoke. "How are you doing?" she asked. The concerned look on her face reflected my exhausted condition.

"Okay. Rough night."

Judy had salt and pepper hair and a reserved but gentle manner. She didn't force conversation, ask endless questions, or constantly scribble notes. Even though her job was to assess and assign resources for families, her attitude was one of genuine compassion and a desire to be helpful. In a few minutes, Judy moved to the floor. We talked about ways in which the therapy helped Baby B, and she offered suggestions regarding his behavior. She also commented on how tired I looked. She had the unique ability to be both personable and professional.

The other services authorized through ECI included occupational therapy (OT) and speech therapy. The purpose of OT was to help Baby B regain body awareness. His spatial regulation (body synchronization of space and pace) had been severely disrupted. So had his sensory deprivation as the result of having been bedridden and on multiple medications. The therapist taught me how to administer exercises to help him get the stimulation and movement he needed throughout the day to reactivate his nerves and muscles.

Although his receptive and expressive speech was severely limited, the speech therapist was impressed with Baby B's ability to follow directions, memorize the alphabet, and mimic sounds and phrases at the age of eighteen months.

"He has an extraordinary memory," she said. "As limb and mobility issues improve, he should be able to devote less time to thinking about his every move and more energy to his cognitive muscle."

One of my favorite activities with Baby B was to read to him. He listened intently and recognized many words by sight. Reading offered us both an escape into the make-believe world of dancing bears, singing birds, and happy children. In the evening when Lawrence arrived home from work, I escaped upstairs to soak in a bath or take a short nap. Later as I prepared dinner, Lawrence sat at the kitchen table with Baby B on his lap for their before-dinner alphabet flash card ritual. Lawrence held up the card; Baby B said the letter and sound: "A-ah." Lawrence flipped the card; Baby B named the picture: "Airplane." Their word play reverberated back and forth like a spiritual chant. We also made sure the closed captioning on the television was enabled so he could hear and see the words.

After dinner, the three of us headed to the family room for floor therapy, a series of activities and interplay techniques to stimulate Baby B's body and mind: bouncing him atop a blue exercise ball, swinging him on a blanket between us, and placing different types of textures in his hands (velvet, satin, sandpaper, bubble wrap) to lessen his fear of touching.

Sometimes as we pushed our way through the nightly procession of therapies, my mind drifted back to evenings

Lawrence and I had spent jogging on neighborhood trails, followed by a quiet dinner and a glass of red wine. Afterward, we would move on to our individual interests and hobbies until bedtime, when we would meet again. We still frequented those same trails when time permitted, but now we walked instead of ran, while we took turns pushing Baby B in his stroller.

We took turns lurching down the hall to extricate Baby B from nightmares that entangled him night after night. At times I wondered if Lawrence ever resented or regretted our loss of freedom. He never said so. I wondered because sometimes I did. These feelings surfaced when I was weighed down by lack of sleep or days confined at home with a toddler and inertia threatened to pull me under.

*   *   *

I needed to locate a pediatric physical therapist quickly. I did not want Baby B to regress because he was no longer attending physical therapy at Shriners. But I had to be sure that I chose correctly. Claire's words replayed in my mind—"There's nobody out there that knows how to provide therapy for burn kids like Shriners."

To add to the urgency, on our last clinic visit, the surgeon had warned me that Baby B had to be walking before more corrective foot surgery could be done. "If he's walking before surgery, he'll try harder to walk after surgery," he said. Fortunately, the therapist at Shriners' child life center also had given me the number of two pediatric therapy clinics in Austin. One fit into my schedule, had experience with burns, and did home therapy.

One sultry summer morning, I opened the door to yet another therapist and was momentarily taken aback. Amanda bore a strong physical resemblance to Claire, Baby B's former physical therapist in Galveston. However, the similarity ended there. From the beginning, Amanda accepted me as a full partner in Baby B's recovery. We agreed on goals and, despite the long road we both knew lay ahead, she was both encouraging and positive. She gently coaxed him to move stiff and sore limbs. Inducing him to walk was our primary goal. Developing scar tissue had left his feet resembling Dutch clogs. Watching his attempts to walk was heartbreaking.

He was also entering the turbulent twos, and I was torn between addressing his challenging behavior or ignoring it altogether. One day I confided to Amanda how distressing it was to make him unhappy when it came to setting limits. "I just want him to be happy and feel loved."

"He's yours now," she said. "You're not going to hurt him. In the end, he will be happier with limits and so will you."

Her words echoed that of Zalena, the nurse at Shriners. "Yours now."

The days morphed into a roiling sea of activity. I spent my days flinging open the front door to a flood of therapists and social workers. I concentrated on staying afloat by envisioning our eventual rescue from this stormy time. I would have welcomed King Kong and a three-ring circus to take up twenty-four-hour residence if they would aid in Baby B's recovery. In my hour of need, I discovered what the poet Rumi expresses. A fortunate person "slips into a house to escape enemies, and opens the doors to the other world."

After the schedule of therapists was firmly in place, I turned my attention to finding a pediatrician. Despite the many disadvantages of my extended stay in Galveston, a major advantage was that I had been less than two miles from Shriners, a medical facility designed for and solely dedicated to meeting the mammoth needs of children with burns. In stark contrast, the nearest children's hospitals to Austin were in Dallas and Houston, each more than three hundred miles away. Also, I found it inconceivable that any local pediatrician would have anywhere near the skill level for treating children with burns as the doctors at Shriners.

I called the Department of Health and Human Services (DHS) for a list of pediatricians who would accept children on Medicaid. I was halfway through calling the seven-page list, and not finding a single doctor who accepted it. Some said they had no idea why they were on the list while others said they were no longer participating. To save time, the first question I asked concerned insurance. Otherwise the scheduler asked a series of questions, made an appointment, and then asked, "Insurance Provider?"

"Medicaid," I replied.

My answer was countered with a terse, "We don't except Medicaid," as if I owed them an apology for wasting their time.

Finally, I found a local clinic that accepted Medicaid and made an appointment. Dr. R's office was located in the corner section of a strip mall that also rented space to a martial arts studio, a real estate office, a resale shop, and a radiology services site. In the waiting room, I sat in one of the plastic chairs scattered around the room on the speckled linoleum floor. Assorted information and flyers printed in English and Spanish were taped to the wall. A plastic children's table and chairs and a blue bin filled with toys and books were in the corner. Two women listlessly watched a *Sesame Street* video on the television mounted on the wall while their toddlers banged on the table with wooden mallets, like natives summoning spirits. When Baby B slapped his hands over his ears, I lifted him from his stroller and sat him on my lap, where his sprawling toddler body pressed me harder into the plastic chair. I turned sideways so that we could look out the window onto the parking lot. "It's okay, it's okay. Look at the cars going by. We'll be back in the car soon."

Eventually we were led into a cluttered, windowless office. All of the high-end symbols of success were absent. The room was clean, lean, and functional, with an examination table pushed against the wall, draped with a single white sheet.

Dr. R, a tall man in his forties with horn-rimmed glasses and grizzled gray hair pulled back in a ponytail, had ditched the traditional white coat in favor of faded jeans and a denim shirt opened at the collar with rolled-up long sleeves. I imagined him once being an idealistic young doctor spending his early career in a third world country, treating malnourished children and coming back to America to treat obese ones.

He introduced himself and offered a seat beside his desk. "I'll just examine him while he sits on your lap," he said, as he pulled his desk chair to face Baby B and me. He gently lifted Baby B's arms and legs and softly traced the trail of scars with his fingers as if he were reading a road map. "Poor little guy," he murmured. I was surprised and touched by his unguarded comment. The medical community cautioned parents to corral grief quickly and come to grips with the new reality that their child's appearance would be forever altered. I appreciated Dr. R's ability to respond with genuine sensitivity.

"You're still being followed by Shriners?" he asked, as he pressed the stethoscope to Baby B's chest.

"Yes, but we need someone locally for routine care and in case we have a problem that needs to be looked at right away, like an infection."

He pushed his chair back and sighed. "Well, we're pretty much run-of-the-mill routine care here. Coughs, colds, making sure kids are up-to-date with their shots, that sort of thing. I haven't had experience with these kind of injuries, so you should probably keep looking for someone with that background, but in the meantime we'll do whatever we can."

I appreciated his candor. I had come in contact with too many doctors exhibiting a bravado way out of proportion to their skill level. Fortunately, a few months later my search led me to Dr. Beth Nauert, a pediatrician experienced with treating traumatized and abused children. I watched the calm, confident way she examined Baby B and answered her measured, probing questions. It was encouraging that she actually listened to my answers. I had been through enough intake interviews to understand that only a sliver of what I said got through. From the beginning Dr. Nauert used a holistic approach in treating Baby B, embracing our family as full partners. She conferred with Kanika on the phone regarding medications that were effective in treating past infections. She never had the attitude of "I'm the doctor; I know what's best." Instead, she actively sought our family's input.

Although I was forced to dive into a sparse and disconnected network of resources on my own, I finally managed to assemble a team of health professionals for Baby B. Yet, they were only a starting lineup that would enter and exit the turnstile of medical and social services that would course in and out of our lives. No one had dared to even give me an estimate of how long and winding the road to recovery would extend. Severe burns in the early stages of injury and age travel an unpredictable path, and the potential for pitfalls is omnipresent.

CHAPTER 26

Dancing Together

"In life as in dance, grace glides on blistered feet."
— *Alice Adams*

A S THE HOT, humid Texas summer advanced, I retreated with Baby B behind closed doors. I had always preferred the early morning freshness of a new day or the breeze that flowed through open windows, but the air outside was stagnant and soaring temperatures soon turned morning dew to afternoon wilt. Air conditioning was no longer optional. In addition to burns having destroyed a significant number of Baby B's sweat glands, the compression burn suit he wore increased the risk of his body overheating. Even walking from a parking lot to a building had become a dangerous undertaking. Staying inside was safest.

There were times that the day crept along like a stalled freight train. On those days I waited for Lawrence to walk through the door so I could escape. I handed over Baby B and got in the car and drove without a destination, until the fog cleared from my brain.

On other days, the present morphed forward at lightning

speed, spiraling through feedings, baths, meds, and therapists coming and going until it seemed as if I were caught up in a time warp.

*   *   *

Miraculously, we were transported into December 2006. Baby B was having his second Christmas with our family, but thankfully we were in Austin, not Galveston. A reporter from the local newspaper, the *Austin-American Statesman*, and I had been in contact regarding her writing a story about Baby B. The reporter, Eileen, and I had been members of an early writing group. I trusted her and felt confident that the story would be written in such a way that would not sensationalize events or violate our privacy. A few days prior to the interview, the paper's photographer arrived to take pictures. She was careful to avoid any facial shots that might compromise Baby B's identity. The following week, Eileen arrived to interview Nicole, Kanika, and me. Lawrence could not be there because of work commitments, but without his dedicated, ongoing presence in my and our daughters' lives, our journey with Baby B would never have been possible. The column and pictures were published just prior to Christmas.

It had been a long time since I had decorated the house for the express purpose of delighting a child. But that Christmas I crawled far back into the closets and pulled out decorations that were favorites of my own children: glittering snow globes, gold stars, and Mr. & Mrs. Santa Claus statues. Silent for a long time, the wound music boxes played "Silent Night" and "Jingle Bells" loud and clear. I purchased extra baubles, twinkling lights, and shiny new bulbs for the tree. Perhaps it was the sights and sounds of the season that changed Baby B from melancholy to merry, but Lawrence and I saw him smile for the first time. The smile spiraled into laughter as he touched tree ornaments and watched as they spun and twinkled. I believed that heaven's angels must have rejoiced also with the sound of his laughter ringing in Christmas Eve. I grabbed a trinket off the tree and dangled it teasingly in front of Baby B as I carried him to Lawrence.

"Let's see how badly he wants this. Hold him up and I'll sit across from you guys." I held up the red and gold gingerbread man and jiggled him. Lawrence slowly let go of his hands. Baby B took two steps forward and suddenly raced toward me. Initially it was the ornament he was after, but when he felt his legs moving he made a wobbly turn and careened around the room with a giddy gusto that reminded me of my own children's first steps. The sheer joy of that moment felt just as magical.

A few weeks later, Baby B and I made the first of many trips back to Shriners for his evaluation at the Shriners clinic. Since he met the prerequisite that he walk prior to foot surgery—"memory imprinting footsteps"—it was time for us to take the next step. Just when our lives seemed manageable, we were forced to return to the world of hospitals, hurt, and doctors. While I dreaded his being subjected to more surgery, I was grateful he had reached a point where it was possible. As his skin healed, it contracted, making his feet less flexible and more misshapen. Without surgery, his gait would become more uneven and rockier, and eventually his ability to walk would cease all together. We always seemed to be weaving in and out of a yin-yang contingency. I had no choice but to carry him across burning coals to get to the other side. Nonetheless, at the thought of his going through another painful surgery, it was my heart, not my feet, that felt as if it were blistering.

Of course, nothing would restore his feet to the baby sweet and soft perfection they surely were, but that he be able to walk was paramount. I often thought about the mother I watched carry her three-year-old son into the open therapy room at

Shriners. His feet had been burned when he stumbled over a smoldering campfire. But there he was running back and forth, circling chairs and tables, laughing so hard he had to stop and start again. The slightly altered shape and the scars scattering the child's naked feet were barely noticeable. *That's going to be Baby B,* I remembered thinking. *Happy and running.*

*   *   *

We were back at the Burn Clinic, a Petri dish for growing anxiety, teemed with activity. The moment I pushed the stroller into the waiting room and witnessed a crowd of children and adults, their faces reflecting my own trepidation, my heart raced and my body tensed. The hours of waiting stretched out as long as a hospital corridor, but finally we reached the end, and the date was set for Baby B's first foot surgery. It would be the first major surgery since his initial life-saving operation. Others would follow—one foot and then the other foot, one hand and then the other hand—in the years to come. We would hope and pray for the best and be thankful when the best was realized. Some surgeries would achieve the desired outcomes. Some fell far short of that goal.

I remained in Galveston for weeks at a time after each surgery to take Baby B to physical therapy and the clinic. Once again, Kanika was coming home after her grueling hospital schedule to assist me with the treatments in order to prevent infections and give fragile skin grafts the best chance of adherence. Lawrence was back to travelling from Austin to Galveston every weekend. Every post-surgery recovery was arduous and toilsome. Wrenching.

One Sunday night after my husband had returned to Austin, I received an unexpected call from my son. At one point, he began to tell me about my grandchildren's current activities and said, "Just so you know—they miss their grandmother." That is when the wall of denial reinforced by isolation broke and the floodgate of tears opened. "I'm sorry," I heard him say through my sobs. "Anything I can do to help?"

"No. Your dad left today; I'm just feeling lonely." The next day my son called and said he was coming to visit for a few days. I was overjoyed when he arrived on Wednesday. He spent the next three days keeping me company and helping me care for Baby B. I was aware that he had major obligations both at home and work. That he had carved out the time to come and comfort me without my asking was a great gift and one I will never forget. My most wonderful memory is of him sitting on the front porch—yes, there are still porches in Galveston—with Baby B on his lap, both enjoying the salt air and afternoon breeze.

* * *

The scrapes and scars from climbing the steep learning curve of caretaking gradually diminished as I navigated my way through new challenges. Because we only returned to Galveston for monthly clinic visits, Kanika was my direct link when I had questions regarding medication and wound care in Austin. She talked me through the times when I felt so overwhelmed that panic threatened to immobilize me. More importantly, contact with Kanika kept Lawrence and me from spending countless hours in crowded emergency rooms for things we could handle at home. Given that Baby B's first line of defense against germs—his skin—was severely damaged, the last place we wanted to place him was in the midst of an emergency room environment teeming with superbugs. Fortunately, in the more than two years that he had lived with us, we endured an emergency room only once, when he had bronchitis. That experience reaffirmed my resolve that emergency rooms would remain a place of last resort.

Nicole kept her promise to help Lawrence and me with Baby B. Even though she was working and pursuing a Master's in Education, she came by often. Additionally, she attended the required foster workshops as preparation for her future role as foster mother and eventually mother. She was learning, just as I had learned, how to salve, wrap, and soothe Baby B's body and psyche. She and I had always had a good relationship, but now that we were in the trenches together, we came to appreciate qualities in each other we might never have discovered otherwise.

We were all pooling together to keep Baby B afloat against a rising tide of ongoing burn-related health issues. Although therapists came routinely, there was no visiting nurse or burn-related specialist I could call with questions.

Ironically, the one agency that should have helped me sort through and find answers to complex care issues was invisible when I needed it. On the contrary, Child Protective Services (CPS) ended up almost destroying the intricate web of love and care our family had managed to weave around Baby B.

CHAPTER 27

Turbulence

"Trouble is like the ocean. It covers two thirds of the earth."

—*Chris Cleave, Little Bee*

ANUARY 2007. CHRISTMAS decorations were shoved to the back of closets. Baby B was napping, and the brilliant afternoon sun shot through the wintery sky, spreading a little strip of sunshine across the rug, the filigree of a branch caught in its radiance. I was in the process of completing yet another monthly report to the Settlement Home for Children detailing my interactions and activities with Baby B. The Settlement Home, a private agency in Austin that managed foster families and adoptions, had contracted with The Children's Center, Inc., the private agency in Galveston supervising Baby B's case, which had contracted with Texas CPS. The shifting of responsibility for foster care children from state to private agencies, according to officials, was intended to save Texas money, reduce state staff, and streamline state services for the children. Instead, it had resulted in a labyrinth of disconnected agencies and authority, and lost and dead children.

I answered the phone on the first ring, not wanting the noise to wake Baby B.

"Hello. I'm calling about Baby B," said the voice on the other end.

I didn't recognize the voice. Not unusual since I received numerous calls from social services regarding him.

"Uh-huh," I replied, still absorbed in filling out reports.

"How's he doing?"

"He's doing fine," I replied, hoping whoever it was would get to the point so that I could finish my paperwork before Baby B woke up.

"Are you still residing at the same Galveston address?"

Must be Shriners. "Yes," I answered. "When we're there for the clinic," I added.

There was an audible silence.

"Is this Kanika?"

"No. This is her mother."

"Where are you?"

At that point, I detected a distinct harshness in the woman's tone.

"Austin," I replied.

"Give me your address!" she ordered.

At that point, I realized it was no ordinary fill-in-the-blanks call. "Just a minute," I replied. "I don't know who you are. I'm not giving you any of my private information until I know what this is about."

She said that she was the Houston CPS worker. Her next words forecast something ominous: "We never had this conversation." The phone clicked, and I realized she had hung up. True to her word, she never called again, but she set in motion a riptide of repercussions that threatened to pull my entire family under.

I immediately called Kanika and told her what had transpired.

"Damn her!" she exclaimed and took a deep breath. "Okay, Mom. I'll call Shirley."

I couldn't remember the last time I actually spoke to Shirley, the Children's Home social worker who had performed the initial foster care intake. Except for an occasional email requesting some report, I hadn't corresponded with her since we had brought Baby B to Austin.

Kanika called me back after talking to her. "The Houston CPS worker and Shirley were not keeping in contact. Now they're blaming each other. It's a mess."

The next day I received the following email from Shirley:

"A lot has transpired since we last spoke regarding Baby B. I do have a lot of concerns about what CPS' plans are. First of all, I will tell you that our agency is in violation because of him residing in Austin."

From there, she went on to enumerate more than a page of infractions that needed to be addressed quickly. And in the next paragraph:

"I know this may seem like a lot. One of two things could happen. CPS could take him away or they will give us a chance to get these things in order."

Finally, she ended the email with this:

"I need to think as to what my plans would be in order to protect Baby B, you, and the Agency."

My mind whirled. *Why did he need protection? He was in a safe, secure, loving home. Why did I need protection for providing that?*

I reread the words with mounting anger, fear, and disbelief. In the coming week I received long, rambling emails from Shirley detailing protocols and procedures she and her agency had failed to implement in their contract with CPS.

After she failed to contact me regarding a home study in Austin, which she told me CPS was requiring, I emailed her:

Have arrangements been made for a home visit to my Austin home this week? I am fearful if this is not done this week, I will open the door and someone will be here to pick up Baby B. How realistic is that?

The next day she emailed me one line: *"I will be arriving tomorrow at 9 a.m."*

I knew our meeting this time would be very different from the initial one two years earlier when she asked me generic questions about my background, marriage, and kids and expressed her appreciation for our commitment to Baby B.

Waiting for her arrival, I tried not to feel resentful. I wondered if she regretted the way she had handled our case. If so, she didn't appear to during her inspection. On that cold January morning, the frosty air followed her through the door and around the house. She carried a clipboard and opened closets (social workers check a child's clothes closet for verification the child is actually residing in the home), checking out bedrooms and bathrooms, peering inside the refrigerator. I half expected her to throw the covers back and look under my bed. Years ago I was a court-appointed children's advocate. This is the protocol for social workers when they monitor parents or caretakers for abuse or neglect.

Really? Me?

Later she sat at the breakfast table and watched as I fed Baby B his oatmeal. It was cozy and warm in the kitchen. To anyone looking in, we could have been friends enjoying morning coffee.

"He's looking good," she said. "A lot different from the last time I saw him."

"It's been a while."

"Yes," she replied. "The last time I saw you, you and your daughter were in Galveston. I always knew you were taking good care of him."

"But CPS didn't?" I asked.

"I was new to the agency," she said. "There were things that should have been done I didn't know about. CPS is doing a lot of threatening and demanding. We're doing our best to satisfy them, but we don't know what they're going to do in the end."

"When are they going to let you know?" I asked.

"A week or two."

As I held Baby B in my arms at the door waiting for her to leave, she said, "Thank you for allowing me into your lovely home."

The next day an email arrived from her with a number of things that needed to be done immediately to bring my home up to "foster care code": electric wall plug-ins, fire extinguishers, and health, fire, and gas inspection and certification. My upper-middle-class neighbors would have been surprised to discover that we were a community of unsafe houses.

And later, another list:

1. A bill with both our names on it (proof we were indeed cohabitants)

2. Two references (proof of our moral fitness)

3. FBI checks (done months previously)

4. Pre-Service foster care training (we had been fostering for two years)

5. W-2 or financial status verification

6. Baby B's doctor documenting: eye, dental, physical, TB

7. TB test for Lawrence and me

8. Marriage license (thirty-five years and counting)

What followed were weeks of frantic calls for appointments and rushing back and forth to fulfill relentless demands. I dreaded clicking on email. *What today?* Lawrence and I hated having to concede our privacy and fingerprints, not knowing where they would end up, but we felt any refusal or resistance would result in Baby B being taken away. And what would become of him after that . . . God only knew. Lost in the system again? But this time forever. The thought was so terrifying that I couldn't give voice to it. It became a silent roiling sea in the pit of my stomach.

CHAPTER 28

Agency Failure

"When the world says, 'Give up,' Hope whispers, 'Try it one more time."

—*Author Unknown*

THE WEEKS CHURNED away. The wave of emails from Shirley halted. A strange silence settled—calm before the storm. I took a deep breath, treading water. One morning, Baby B was slapping his bath water, delighting in the currents he caused. I liked bathing him in the guest bathroom. Unlike the master bath, it was small and cozy, cocoon-like. Before Kanika left for college, it was filled with teenage girl things. Now a yellow rubber ducky floated on the water, and a green frog that squirted water from its red tongue sat on the tub rim.

Baby B was slowly becoming acclimated to baths. There was still a moment just before I slipped him in that I felt a slight resistance—I'd hold my breath—until he trusted and let go. Each time it happened I felt a gush of gratitude so great I thought I would burst. It happened that morning—just before the tsunami erupted.

As I prepared to lift Baby B out of the water, my cell began to buzz on the bathroom counter. It was always within reaching distance for fear I might miss an important call from social services. I dropped the towel and sat on the edge of the tub, swirling the bath water around Baby B with my free hand.

"Mrs. Bowen, good morning; this is Shirley."

Her voice had a sober, foreboding sound—one you hope never to hear in the middle of the night. But it was morning, and the sun was shining.

"Mrs. Bowen, I'm sorry but CPS is ordering us to pick up Baby B tomorrow."

How do you describe the moment you receive news over the phone that is so devastating your mind disengages from your body?

"What? What did you say? That doesn't make sense. What did we do wrong? Nobody can take care of him and love him the way we do. I can't believe this."

"Yes, I know," said Shirley. "We told them that you were the best place for him. But we've done all we can. I'm making plans to fly in tomorrow. Please have him ready."

She hung up.

Trembling so badly I was afraid I might drop him, I removed Baby B from his bath, crying silently as I dried him and dressed his wounds, then carried him downstairs for his breakfast. I struggled to remain calm, knowing how sensitive he was to my emotional state. He often seemed to test the temperature of his environment, using me as a touchstone. I walked a tightrope of self-control to steady him. His big brown eyes were locked like lasers on me. I held him close to comfort myself as well as him.

When he was safely settled in his high chair, sipping juice, I called Lawrence at work and told him about the call. "Come home right away."

*   *   *

We stood in the kitchen, our arms encircling each other.

"I'm sorry," he whispered. "What do you want me to do?"

"Take care of Baby B," I said, my voice shaking. "I've got to make some calls . . . try to find somebody who might know someone I can call to stop this."

I plowed through my list of cell phone contacts and tapped the number of anyone who might be able to give me advice. I was diligent about maintaining the names of therapists, social service contacts, and parents who were especially helpful in sharing information about available medical resources for Baby B.

I called one person after another and retold the story, as quickly and succinctly as possible, of CPS' plans to take Baby B from us in less than twenty-four hours. Time was running out. It was late Friday afternoon, and even if I obtained the name of someone who could stop CPS, they might already have left.

Everyone I called expressed shock and disbelief: *Can't believe . . . I wish I could help, but . . . have you tried . . .*

There were only a few people left on the list. *What else could I do? What if Baby B and I were gone when Shirley arrived?* Would she call the police?

I didn't realize I was gripping the cell phone and envisioning running away with Baby B until it rang. The screen displayed Judy, the Early Childhood Intervention coordinator's number, one of the people I had already called.

"Cynthia," she said, "I have the number of someone who might be able to help you."

I dialed the number and held my breath. On the second ring, a woman answered. I was taken back by the incredible gentleness of her voice. I had expected a terse tone along the lines of *"Don't you know it's Friday afternoon. Everyone has already left. Call back Monday."* But of course by Monday, Baby B would be gone.

However, this wonderful woman listened to me ramble on

half hysterical and crying. She took the information she needed to confirm my story and said, "Stay by the phone. I'll call you back."

Leaning on the kitchen counter, I continued to grip my cell, ready to punch the button, like a contestant on a game show. My heart pounded.

Thankfully, it didn't take long.

"We've determined it's an agency failure, not a foster family failure," she said.

"You mean CPS is not going to take him away tomorrow?"

"No," she said. "We've talked to them."

"So I don't have to worry about a sheriff or someone at my door tomorrow taking him away?" I had seen those television scenes of babies being pulled from the arms of women who loved them.

"No," she said. "That won't happen."

"Thank you, thank you," I said.

"You're welcome," she replied.

I glanced at the clock. At four-thirty on Friday, the nightmare ended. I raced upstairs to tell Lawrence.

*   *   *

It turned out that the woman who had responded so quickly to my call was Mary Jo, an official from the office of Senator Steve Ogden. Because of the quick reaction of dedicated people, beginning with Judy Wade, Baby B and our family were spared the tragic consequences of an "agency failure."

Later, I wrote Senator Ogden the following:

I want to thank you, Senator Ogden, and your assistant, Mary Jo, for intervening so quickly to prevent Baby B from being removed from our home that bleak, cold Friday. It still scares me to think where Baby B might be today if your office had not responded as quickly as it did. As Mary Jo said, "It was an agency failure not a foster home failure."

The Settlement House is our new foster care agency in Austin. They have done an excellent job to make sure our home meets state requirements. We have been fingerprinted, submitted financial statements, driver licenses, and social security numbers. Friends, family, and relatives have been interviewed. In short, like other foster families, we have given up basic privacy freedoms in order to love and care for a needy child. One day we hope to adopt Baby B into our family.

On April 21, 2007, the Senate voted 29-2 to give private firms and the Department of Health and Human Services funding and broader authority to get children into foster care. If it had not been for your intervention, both of these entities would have failed our family and my foster child. I pray that no child will ever be removed from a caring, devoted family because of these agencies' failure to cooperate with each other in the best interest of the child. If I had it within my power, I would pass a Baby B Resolution to remind agencies of the awesome obligation they have to "first do no harm" to children.

Again, thank you and your office for your quick response to prevent what would have been a tragic removal from our home for a child that has already been through unspeakable horror."

I hoped some official would call and admit that their CPS social worker had tried to conceal the fact that she had lost track of a foster child—that she had attempted to hide that fact by terrorizing our family and trying to tear Baby B away from a loving family. No one called.

With the threat of CPS to take Baby B no longer lingering

over us like a drone, I forged ahead. It had been two years of hard-won lessons. I intended to stay on top of things. Prepare for the unexpected. Trust but verify. I leaned into a pessimism that threatened to tip to paranoia at any point.

I began to keep a journal and documented every conversation, every correspondence, every appointment, and every meeting that I had with anyone involving foster care, CPS, and social services. I never ended any conversation without confirming the person's name and phone number and noting the date and time. That same month, a two-page article appeared in the *Austin-American Statesman* entitled "Child care reforms overwhelm foster care."

I clipped newspaper articles about families involved in disputes with CPS. When one file filled, I began another. I feared becoming a paper hoarder. Mostly, I felt like David from the Bible, piling up little nuggets of protection. The next time Goliath stomped into my home, I would pull out the file drawer labeled "FIGHT!" and fling stacks of paper at the giant.

It was not until Nicole adopted Baby B that I stopped arming myself with paper. Before the adoption was finalized, however, there was one more monster to slay.

CHAPTER 29

Mississippi Calling

"We've come a long way, but the journey is not complete."
—Anonymous

Aᴜɢᴜsᴛ 2007, 4 a.m. On a hot, muggy morning, Kanika and I carried our suitcases out the door. The street was dark and deserted. A single car passed, catching us in its headlights as we moved stealth-like through the thick air.

If you have ever stood in the middle of the desert at night and marveled at the vastness of the sky, you might have some idea of what it felt like to stand on an island at dawn and look heavenward at the moon. The snow-white orb illuminated the street, and the beams reflected off the shimmering sea. I took in the spectacle one last time before I stepped into the car.

We were leaving Texas to travel to a place I could not have conjured up in my wildest imagination ever going: *Mississippi.* I knew little about the state except what I had read in history books and newspapers or had seen on the news. Not much of it was positive. This, however, was 2007, not 1965. Two African-American women travelling alone through the Deep South no longer was considered dangerous. We would be gone for a week,

the longest I had ever been away from Baby B, although leaving
him in the loving hands of Nicole and Lawrence allowed me to
go without worry.

We were travelling to the trial of the woman accused of
nearly taking Baby B's life. For reasons I could not fathom, it
had taken over two years for authorities to bring her to trial. In
the beginning, knowing that she remained free even as Baby B
remained imprisoned in a body disfigured and wracked by pain
enraged me. That rage was slowly sapping me of the strength I
needed to give myself fully to him. Eventually, I realized that
each minute I gave her a thought was a minute stolen from him.
I made a vow not to allow her to take a single thing more from
him.

*   *   *

I enjoyed road trips with Kanika. When she was in college, we
took road trips to Dallas to visit my son and his family or went
sightseeing to funky art communities surrounding Austin with
the car top down and the tunes thumping. It occurred to me that
it had been a long time since I had listened to any music other
than soothing classical that calmed Baby B. When I listened to
her eclectic music collection of CDs of Bob Marley and the Dave
Matthews Band, I felt fragments of a buried joy resurfacing.
Neither of us needed to crowd the car with chatter. We were
very much alike in that way, preferring private thoughts to a
parade of words.

As we drove through Louisiana on Interstate 10, I saw the
imprint of watermarks on buildings from Hurricane Katrina. In
August 2005, I had been twisting in the throes of my new life with
Baby B. I could not bear to watch news reports of the suffering
that surfaced during and in the aftermath of the hurricane.

*   *   *

Kanika pulled into the town square of Holly Springs, Mississippi, in the late afternoon. We exited the car and stood in silence. Afternoon activity swirled all around us. The sunshine was so bright that the trees, grass, and buildings were enveloped in a hazy translucence. White fluffs from cottonwood trees floated on heat waves like tiny apparitions.

The buildings lining the square were in the high Italianate revival mode characteristic of post-Civil War architecture. At each cornerstone was the state flag emblazoned with the Confederate battle flag's saltire flapping in the breeze. Occasionally I saw Confederate flag emblems in Texas on bumper stickers, caps, clothing, and body tattoos, but never as part of the flag. Mississippi is the sole state that chose to make it an official part of the state flag.

Kanika and I advanced up a walkway leading to the center of the square, where an antebellum courthouse sat in stately splendor. Four white columns fronted the building like centurions. A massive clock with a face of Roman numerals crowned the tower. Voices from inside a white gazebo drifted across the expansive green lawn. *Hadn't I seen this setting in some opening movie scene?*

Inside the courthouse, the person who had arranged our accommodations and would act as liaison for the court proceedings waited. A tall, blond, blue-eyed woman glided toward us and greeted us with all the charm and personality of a former Miss Mississippi. "Y'all made it. Did you have a good drive? Didn't get lost or anything?" Her smile was wide and welcoming.

"No, we drove straight through; no problems," Kanika replied, her smile equally generous.

"Well, my name is Colleen, and I'm going to be showing y'all around while you're here, lettin' you know when you need to be in court and such."

"Hi, I'm Cynthia Bowen, and this is my daughter, Kanika."

"The mama and the little girl," she exuded, placing one hand on my shoulder and the other on Kanika's. She stated this with all the delight of having discovered a matching set. Either this was the southern version of the handshake or we had just been anointed. For the next three days, with every introduction, that was how she referred to Kanika and me: "The mama and the little girl." I found great pleasure in reminding Kanika that even though she was the doctor, I was the mama and she was still the little girl.

As the three of us were about to exit the courthouse, a man approached. Picture the Marlboro man from the cigarette commercial era—six feet tall, cowboy hat and boots, handsome and rugged.

"This is my husband, the sheriff," said Colleen.

Standing side by side, they *were* a match.

"I'm going to take them over to check in; I'll see you at supper," she told him.

Colleen led us across the street where a phalanx of small shops lined the block. We walked up the side stairs to the second floor of a recently renovated building onto a balcony leading to the Court Square Inn, where she had reserved a two-bedroom suite for us. The room was stately and spacious, but with a coziness that chain hotel rooms never manage to achieve.

After walking through the rooms with us, she paused at the door. "It's pretty isolated around here at night once all the shops close," she said. "If you need anything or you hear anything and get scared, you call me right away. Don't worry 'bout wakin' me up. I'll have my husband out of bed and over here before you know it." She paused again, sizing up Kanika and me with genuine concern. I was touched by her sincerity. Yet, I couldn't think of anything scarier than what I had already experienced, given the tragedy that brought me to this place.

"Don't worry, we will," I assured her as she walked out the door.

We left briefly before nightfall to buy take-out. Back in the room, we ate, watched local TV news, and leafed through town magazines. The square was indeed deserted and steely silent. Apparently we were the only occupants at the inn. We hadn't heard anyone walking along the balcony leading to the other two suites, and ours was the only car parked below. I peeked out the curtain and saw there was just enough light from the street lamps to cast menacing shadows over the sidewalks.

Around 9:30 p.m. we heard a series of short car horn blasts followed by dogs howling. Kanika and I looked at each other. *What the . . . ?* We parted the window drapes. Idling on the street below was a white Hummer. Colleen was at the wheel. We opened the door and walked out onto the balcony and waved to her.

"Y'all doin' all right?" she asked. The dogs continued to bark, their heads hanging out the back windows. "Those are my huntin' hounds."

"Oh, they're cute. We're fine," I replied, touched again by her regard for our safety.

"You got a gun?" she inquired.

"A gun?" I repeated.

"Yeah," she said.

"No. We don't have a gun," I replied.

"You ain't got a gun?" She asked the question with the incredulity you would say to your smelly teenager who has just exited the shower: "You didn't use soap?"

She eyed us with a look of bafflement. "Well, see ya in the mornin'. Call me if you need anything."

We watched the Hummer roll slowly down the street, while the dogs howled, and turn a corner before we rushed back inside.

We rechecked the time the trial was to begin the next morning, watched the last of the nightly news, and retired to our separate bedrooms. It had been a long drive and a long day. The district attorney had said there was a possibility that as the foster mother for the past two years, I might be called as a witness. I wanted to be well rested so that I could give a clear accounting of Baby B's ongoing fight to recover from life-threatening injuries.

CHAPTER 30

The Trial

*"Not everything that is faced can be changed but nothing
is changed if not faced."*

—James Baldwin

OURTROOMS—NO MATTER WHERE the location—are by
design and function intimidating and uncomfortable.
The Holly Springs courtroom was no different. The
high white walls and ceiling were in sharp contrast to the dark
wood color of the spectator seats. A drab runner rug divided
the left and right gallery sections where spectators could sit in
individual, hard-molded, auditorium-like seats.

However, the only thing I felt as I sat in the antiquated
surroundings was a sense of urgency and determination that
the terrible things Baby B had endured be acknowledged. The
time was way overdue for the person responsible for inflicting
permanent injuries to his little body be brought to justice.

Kanika and I sat on the left side of the courtroom behind
the railing that separated spectators from the lawyers, jury, and
judge. We were several rows behind the prosecutors, District
Attorney Ben Creekmore and Assistant DA Lani Hill. I looked

behind us and saw that except for a newspaper reporter and a victim's rights advocate, and a few people I didn't recognize, every seat was vacant. That both surprised and saddened me. I wanted to believe that people in his home state remembered Baby B and cared about what had happened to him.

I looked across the room to where the defense lawyer, John Dolan, sat next to his client. I wanted to see *her* face, but his frame blocked my view. His client was at the center of my nightmares. I felt that if I could put a face to those terrifying dreams, I might once again be able to look forward to a peaceful night's sleep.

Why had she chosen to go to trial rather than accept the plea bargain of felony child neglect she was offered? Did she think that she bore no responsibility? Had she convinced herself that being free for so long meant no one cared enough to prosecute?

The jury sat to the left, eight women and four men, looking sober and ready. The bailiff called the court to order. Presiding Judge Howorth, a tall man wearing horn-rimmed glasses, strode into court and sat on the bench. He was as confident and relaxed as if he were sitting at the head of a dinner table.

I could see the backs of Creekmore and Hill at the prosecution table. Hill had been deliberate in making sure the case came to trial. Someone had said that she had a child about the age of Baby B, as well as five other children. She stood for a moment before the jury ready to make the opening argument. Her blond hair fell loosely to her shoulders. She wore a basic business suit, sensible and functional. She expressed sympathy for everything Baby B had been through, saying she had six children, one about the age of Baby B. She said the defendant had given two different versions of how the incident happened—once blaming his two-year-old brother, next blaming a fourteen-year-old visitor.

One by one, witnesses took the stand to testify about screams coming from the apartment that July evening. The sirens. The ambulance.

A police investigator took the stand. "The defendant," he said, nodding toward the woman, "has given conflicting statements to law enforcement and other agencies. She admits he was scalded, but always deflected blame from herself."

Dr. S, the staff physician from Shriners who had been Baby B's admitting doctor, provided the expert testimony. With the same precise, restrained manner he had displayed at Shriners, Dr. S said, "The contours and burn patterns on Baby B were consistent with being immersed in scalding water."

"Can you show the jury what position Baby B would have been in when he was immersed?" asked the prosecutor. The jury was allowed to stand up and shift into position for a clear view. The spectators behind the railings leaned forward quietly, their necks straining. Then all sound and movement ceased, as if the entire courtroom were captured, frozen in action.

All eyes were on Dr. S as he positioned himself on the floor, his legs spread straight out in front. He leaned forward to simulate Baby's position in the bathtub that evening. Then he stood up and, while bending over with his arms extended, he explained. "You can see how the defendant's hands would have pressed down on Baby B from behind."

The prosecutor paced the floor. "Dr. S, would you show us one more time how the defendant would have had to hold the child down? We want the jury to have a clear understanding of the defendant's actions."

The defense objected.

Judge Howorth overruled the objection.

The prosecutor asked Dr. S about the defendant's demeanor while she was at Shriners.

"The defendant didn't seem all that worried. She left the hospital while Baby B was in surgery. Whenever she was in his room, the child became significantly more agitated and required medication to calm him."

The state-appointed defense attorney, John Dolan, was of average height with dark hair beginning to gray and recede at the hairline. He rose to cross-examine Dr. S. "So are you an expert on the bath behaviors of young children?" he asked

Dr. S replied, "No, but I have young children of my own, and I give them baths." He looked directly at Dolan. "No child could have sustained injuries to the extent of Baby B's without force being applied."

At last, the court called me to the witness stand. I felt as if I had been holding my breath the entire time. My heart pounded as I raised my right hand to take the oath. The first thing I did after sitting down was look at my daughter. When our eyes met, I felt emboldened.

Finally, I had a clear view of the defendant. She was looking directly at me—smiling. She was an attractive woman with dark shoulder-length hair framing soft curls around her face— and big brown eyes. She looked nothing like the woman in my nightmares. I met her gaze and looked away.

DA Creekmore asked me a series of questions about the two years I had been Baby B's foster mother. *Describe a typical day. What kind of pain was he in? Describe Shriners' tub room.*

I remembered telling Kanika once in a fit of fury that I wished she had prepared me better for the tub room.

"*Nothing*," she said, "can prepare you for the tub room."

He asked me to identify photographs of Baby B's scorched body.

"In the entire time you were foster mother, did the defendant ever contact you to see how Baby B was doing?" he asked.

"No. Never."

He asked me how it felt to care for a critically ill child.

"He is labor of love seven days a week, twenty-four hours a day," I replied.

Creekmore presented photographs to the court for the jury to see. Dolan made a request to view the photos first.

Creekmore crossed the room and handed them to Dolan. Dolan shifted through the pictures and slid them across the table to his client. She glimpsed at them as casually as if she were glancing at a supermarket magazine. The smile was gone but nothing replaced it—no hint of recognition. No sign of sorrow.

The defense lawyer objected to the pictures being given to the jury on the grounds they might be prejudicial. Judge Howorth overruled the objection.

The photos passed from juror to juror. I looked at their faces as they examined the pictures. Some frowned; others pressed their lips together and shook their heads. Some shuffled through them while others only looked at a few and passed them along.

The defense called only one witness, the maintenance worker at the apartments, who testified he had not seen the defendant previously abuse her child.

The defendant chose not to take the stand.

* * *

On the third day of the trial, DA Creekmore stepped from behind the defense table and stood in front of the jury to give closing arguments. He began by saying that he had three children. He shook his head. "It's extraordinarily difficult to look at those photos and not imagine the suffering." He paused for a moment. "We know child abuse occurs. And we all, as parents, have stresses. That's not an excuse."

"There were three witnesses." He held up a finger as he identified each one. "Baby B, the defendant's two-year-old son, and the defendant." He pointed at the defendant. "The blame is right there."

He adjusted his tie and put both hands in his suit pockets. Then he took them out and rubbed his palms together.

He recounted the multiple surgeries Baby B had been through and reminded the jury about Dr. S' testimony about the location of pain receptors near the skin's surface, which intensified Baby B's suffering every day. Then he added, "The rest of the story in this case is that those with pain receptors stepped up and helped: the doctors, the nurses, his foster family."

He turned and pointed at the defendant. "There is one who had no pain receptors in this case and that's that monster over there!"

All eyes shifted to the defendant.

I flinched at the word 'monster' to describe her. Yes, she had done a monstrous thing, but she was still a human being. She was once someone's little girl, someone's friend, someone with a future. She had given birth to the child that I now loved.

Over the span of years to where she now sat at the age of twenty-three, something had gone terribly wrong, and Baby B had paid the price. Regardless of her outside demeanor, she had to be horrified at what she had become—what she had done. Perhaps the only way she kept her sanity was by cementing a wall around herself. When that wall crumbled, she might be able to reclaim her humanity.

Defense attorney Dolan approached the jury slowly as if he were taking a thoughtful stroll. His closing argument highlighted the defendant as an impoverished single mother dealing with challenging circumstances. That she loved her children and had possibly made poor choices. That something tragic had occurred. That no witnesses were present. That she should be given the benefit of the doubt.

*   *   *

The judge instructed the jury to consider a lesser charge of felony child neglect if it did not have sufficient evidence to arrive at a guilty verdict on the felony child abuse charge.

The trial lasted three days, and on a sweltering August afternoon, the verdict: Felony Child Abuse.

When Judge Howorth announced the sentence—twenty years—the defendant collapsed back into her chair, sobbing.

"I'm too young to go to prison!" she screamed.

Those were her only words and her only emotional display since the trial's inception. Perhaps the first crack in the wall had surfaced.

Kanika and I held on to each other in a long embrace. We turned and watched as bailiffs ordered Faye to stand, handcuffed her hands behind her back, and led her away.

CHAPTER 31

We Are Family

"And I could see that it was about tragedy transformed over the years into joy. It was about the beauty of sheer effort."

— *Anne Lamott*

TWO YEARS LATER on April 7, 2009, I returned to court. This time, however, it was a family court in Texas, bright and modern and filled with people. People were there for all kinds of reasons. Some were fighting to keep their families from being torn asunder. Some had lost the fight and were going through the ritual of surrender. Then there were families who had come for the same reason as ours—to publicly declare their devotion to a new family member.

Although my daughter, Nicole, was officially declared Baby B's mother that day, in every way that truly counted she had already been fulfilling that role as his foster mother until the adoption was finalized. She had never wavered in her desire to commit to him fully, even though she too had encountered the rocky road of social services oversight: home study, agency compliances and contradictions, and FBI fingerprinting. Fortunately, since I had already paved the way as his first foster mother, her journey was not as strewn with booby traps.

Baby B had suffered many losses in many ways, but the family that surrounded him would do battle to make sure those losses did not define his future. Nicole, Kanika, and I carried the superpower of three mothers. My husband, Lawrence, Baby B's constant companion, packed the power of a superhero. As I reached up to touch Baby B's beautiful face, I recalled the words of Mother Teresa: "The problem with the world is that we draw the circle of our family too small."

*   *   *

The Bowen family was called to come forth into the court well. Baby B, perched on Lawrence's shoulders, looked happily down on us all. He loved riding on my husband's shoulders with his little arms wrapped around his "Papa." I looked at my husband and thought how perfectly the inscription I had seen on a Shriners van fit him: *It takes a man to bend down and lift a child onto his shoulders.*

My daughters stood on each side of me. Kanika on my left had brought Baby B into our family. Nicole on my right had committed to making sure he remained forever.

Sally, the foster care director for The Settlement Home for Children, a respected children's home and foster care agency that had guided us through the final adoption process, joined our circle.

The judge presiding, the Honorable Don Higginbotham, stepped down from his bench to complete the circle. He declared:

It is now hereby Ordered, Adjudged and Decreed that

Baby B Bowen
Is Declared to be the child of,
And it is further Declared that said child is a
member of the
Nicole A. Bowen
Family, with all the rights and responsibilities
attached thereto.

Epilogue

"I know the plans I have for you, declares the Lord, plans to prosper you and not to harm you, plans to give you hope and future.

—Bible, Jeremiah 29:11

THE TERRIFIED TODDLER who used to clamp his hands over his ears at sudden sounds is now a ten-year-old at the piano playing the beginning stanzas of "Happy" by Pharrell Williams. Because Baby B has perfect pitch, he has the ability to identify or re-create any given musical note by ear. After numerous operations, hands that were once so constricted by burn tissue they could barely hold a baby cup can now riff on the piano. With hands that scars cannot silence, he performs solo concerts at school, church, and nursing homes.

The hurting toddler who once could barely hobble across the room because of the injuries to his legs and feet has won Special Olympics medals for basketball and bowling.

He has risen from each assault to his body, stronger and more determined. His body ripples with "honors given out after battle, small triumphs pinned to the chest."

Several years ago Baby B was diagnosed with autism. Our family calls it "awesomeness." Like many children on the autism spectrum, he has significant strengths and significant challenges. While he is gifted musically and has pockets of brilliance academically, he struggles with verbal, social, and comprehension skills. We accept and love him through it all. In the end, he is no different than any other child needing guidance and unconditional love. What child doesn't need those things?

It had been eight years since I spoke to that little girl in the elevator at Shriners Hospital. At that time she looked to be around nine years old, which means now she would be entering adulthood. I hope that life has been kind to her and all the other brave children and parents I met in the years that Baby B received treatment at Shriners. I hope that most scars have faded along with the worst of their memories. I hope that whatever remains, whether it be memories or scars, serves as a testament to their will to survive and their strength to persevere.

In June 2007, our prayers were answered when Dell Children's Medical Center of Central Texas opened in Austin. With its multidisciplinary team of pediatric specialists and nurses located near us, we no longer had to travel to Galveston for the surgeries Baby B required.

Over the years, I have spent hundreds of hours in hospital and therapy waiting rooms. We parents and grandparents and caretakers live in a watch and wait euphoria. We are in a perpetual state of active, hopeful wait. No matter what the neurologists, psychologists, surgeons, teachers, or therapists predict, we see hope fulfilled in ways they cannot. In a look. In a word. In a kiss.

Nicole and I have been forceful enough and fortunate enough over the years to have those in the medical and the educational sphere listen to us when we tell them what Baby B—the individual—needs.

Because of the Individuals with Disabilities Education Act (IDEA), children with special needs are no longer warehoused or denied an equal education. Not only do they benefit by learning in a typical environment, their peers' education is also enhanced because they make friends with children with whom they might not otherwise interact.

Today I look back in amazement at what our family accomplished. Most of all, I marvel at what a blessing Baby B has been to each one of us. In a very short time, he became a testament to what we could not have learned any other way: the mystery of the family we are born into and the miracle of the family we create.

Acknowledgments

FIRST OF ALL, I would like to express my gratitude to Shriners Hospital for Children (Galveston) for saving Baby B's life and the caring, dedicated staff for their support during my extended visits. Also I am forever thankful to:

Dr. Beth Nauert, the wonderful pediatrician who we were fortunate enough to find on our return to Austin.

Dell Children's Medical Center in Austin where each hospital stay Baby B was surrounded with tender, loving, care by compasionate nurses and staff

Dr. Steven Henry, Baby B's plastic surgeon, a miracle worker

Dr. Dilip Karnik and his holistic approach to treating autism

Texas Scottish Rite Hospital for picking up the ball when others dropped it

Early Childhood Intervention for helping Baby B and me through those early hard years

Meredith Hamons, the music therapist who extracts music magic from Baby B

Special Olympics and their extraordinary volunteers

Autism Society of Central Texas

Numerous speech, physical, and occupational therapists through the years.

Grateful for these lights that shined my way: Megan Arnold, Ms. Jackie, Amanda Lutz, Amanda Brown May, Sharon O'Connell, Amy Ray, Judy Wade, Kim Wirth

Like Baby B, this book has been a labor of love. I thank my early writing groups and the last best, Novelcrafters.

CPSIA information can be obtained
at www.ICGtesting.com
Printed in the USA
BVOW11s1915230316

441525BV00014B/186/P